CITIZENSHIP, INEQUALITY, AND DIFFERENCE

THE LAWRENCE STONE LECTURES

Sponsored by:

The Shelby Cullom Davis Center for Historical Studies
and Princeton University Press
A list of titles in this series appears at the back of the book.

Citizenship, Inequality, and Difference

HISTORICAL PERSPECTIVES

Frederick Cooper

PRINCETON UNIVERSITY PRESS

PRINCETON & OXFORD

Copyright © 2018 by Princeton University Press

Published by Princeton University Press,
41 William Street, Princeton, New Jersey 08540

In the United Kingdom: Princeton University Press,
6 Oxford Street, Woodstock, Oxfordshire OX20 1TR

press.princeton.edu

All Rights Reserved

ISBN 978-0-691-17184-5

LCCN 2017958892

British Library Cataloging-in-Publication Data is available

Editorial: Brigitta van Rheinberg and Amanda Peery
Production Editorial: Debbie Tegarden
Jacket art courtesy of Shutterstock
Production: Erin Suydam
Publicity: James Schneider
Copyeditor: Jodi Beder

This book has been composed in Miller

Printed on acid-free paper. ∞

Printed in the United States of America

10 9 8 7 6 5 4 3 2 1

CONTENTS

THIS BOOK ORIGINATES in the Lawrence Stone Lectures, sponsored by the Davis Center for Historical Studies of Princeton University and Princeton University Press. They were delivered in April 2016. There is nothing like preparing for well-publicized lectures before an audience of highly accomplished scholars to add an element of fear to the usual inducements to intellectual initiative. In speaking before an audience of historians who covered all time periods and all parts of the globe, I sought to look beyond my own area of specialization in the history of French Africa. This self-imposed task took me to many places where I was skating on very thin ice. The lectures were based less on my research than on making the connection between issues that came up in my work and a wider and more varied literature. The Princeton audience was as courteous as it was intellectually rigorous, so this project benefitted greatly from the route it took from conception to book.

Freed in the book version from the constraint of packing 2000 years of globe-spanning history into three fifty-minute lectures, I have elaborated on important points and, in the notes, given credit where credit is due—which is essentially everywhere. But I have tried not to stray too far from the idea of the Lawrence Stone Lectures, turning the lecture format into a reflective essay. This is not a comprehensive study of citizenship in world history. It is a small book on a big topic, and if it provokes more questions than it answers, then it will have met one of my goals. It is an engagement with some essential themes in the study of citizenship—in past and present—and it relies on select examples. The nature of the topic means crossing different literatures, not just the divisions of the historical profession by time and place, but ventures into political theory, legal studies, sociology, and anthropology.

For me, and I hope for the reader, one of the most stimulating challenges of the project was to put the political ethnography and history of Africa into conversation with other historical domains and to explore the confrontation of polities whose conception of political belonging were quite different. Each of these domains has been the life work of excellent scholars, and if coming to grips with any one of them entails simplification, bringing them into conversation offers possibilities of thinking across time and space, as many political actors and thinkers have done across the centuries.

Fortunately, when I was preparing the lectures, I had the benefit of the support of two institutions that gave me time and resources to undertake extensive reading and reflection. During the academic year 2015–16, I was a fellow of the research group on "Labor and Life Course in Global History," more commonly known as "re:work," at the Humboldt University in Berlin. I profited greatly from the insights of my fellow fellows, of the director Andreas Eckert, and of other scholars in Berlin associated with re:work. The staff, ably led by Felicitas Hentschke, provided much more than the support that I and the other fellows needed to get our work done; they also provided a congenial and stimulating atmosphere. My second home in Berlin was the Wissenschaftskolleg zu Berlin, where my spouse Jane Burbank was a fellow. Wiko, as it calls itself, is as kind to partners as it is to fellows, with the added benefit of imposing no obligations. Since I did much of my work in our apartment in the Wiko complex, I made extensive use of the Wiko library services. The librarians fetched books from libraries all around Berlin and beyond. I am very grateful to the head librarian, Sonja Grund, and her staff for meeting my extensive demands—probably as great as those of any of the official fellows—with the utmost courtesy and efficiency. And a word of thanks to the rector Luca Giuliani—and through him the rest of the Wiko staff—for making this such a supportive place to work. I would also like to thank members of the Wiko community for many enlightening conversations, and particularly a group of them who let me present to them a dress rehearsal for the three lectures and gave me useful—and occasionally sharp—feedback that improved the clarity of the lectures and of this book: Michael Gordin, Erika Milam, Hassan Jabareen, Rina Rosenberg, and Jane Burbank. I also received helpful comments from a presentation of some of my lecture material to the re:work fellows shortly before the Princeton lectures, and I benefitted from many conversations at re:work throughout the year.

I am very grateful to my hosts at Princeton for inviting me and organizing every aspect of the lectures in thoughtful way. I was first approached by Brigitta van Rheinberg, Director of Global Development and History Publisher at the Press, whom I already knew from preparing the book *Empires in World History* that I coauthored with Jane Burbank. I appreciate her confidence in me and am grateful for her encouragement to take on a topic that strayed well beyond my comfort zone. Philip Nord, head of the Davis Center, was also responsible for the invitation and was a thoughtful host in Princeton as well as an insightful critic. Brigitta, Phil, and Adam Beaver gave me warm introductions at the three lectures and were excellent companions throughout the visit. I am most of all grateful to members of the Princeton faculty, graduate students, and visitors who attended lectures at a busy time of the year—in many cases all three of them on consecutive days—and whose questions and comments were extremely helpful in the writing of this book. The next to last draft of the introduction benefitted from a close reading at a seminar with the Global Studies Center of the University of Pittsburgh. Over the years, different aspects of my work on citizenship, especially in relation to French Africa, have been presented at many conferences and lectures, and discussions of these presentations have influenced the present publication. The two anonymous readers for the Press provided very helpful comments for the final round of revisions. Danielle Beaujon meticulously checked the accuracy of footnotes and quotations. A special word of thanks to Jane Burbank for her careful and sensitive reading of the manuscript of this book.

Translations of quotations from French sources are my own unless otherwise noted.

—*New York, September 2017*

CITIZENSHIP, INEQUALITY, AND DIFFERENCE

Citizenship and Belonging

IN THE FALL OF 2015, as I began work on the project that became this book, tens of thousands of people from Syria, Afghanistan, Eritrea, and elsewhere were streaming into Europe, struggling through the rain and cold, on foot or in small boats, trying to enter the European Union. They were skirting some borders and crossing others. Many were fleeing Syria, where a government was willing to destroy cities and citizens to preserve the power of a ruling clique, abetted by other factions within the territory and external allies. A smaller number of young men were moving in the opposite direction, to leave their countries of citizenship to join the Islamic State, a political entity of unclear dimensions that had conquered territory in Iraq and Syria and pretended to be the echo of the caliphates that began in the seventh century. Some European states built walls—literally—to keep out people who had lost the protection of their own citizenship. Germany was torn between those who believed it could and should take in large numbers of asylum seekers and those who saw a threat to their sense of Germanness. This debate was taking place in relation to one of the world's most innovative citizenship regimes: a person's citizenship in a national state automatically conveys a European citizenship that recognizes his or her right to live and work as a rights-bearing citizen throughout the European Union. That regime is becoming increasingly precarious in the face of conflicting views, inclusionary and exclusionary, of citizenship. Meanwhile, states that are not so wealthy and without such a deep democratic history—Jordan, Lebanon, Turkey—are shouldering an even bigger burden of housing and caring for Syrian refugees.

In the fall of 2016, as I continued to work on this manuscript, American voters chose as their president a man who proposes to build a wall to keep Mexicans out of the United States and deport millions who are already here, who conflates Muslims with terrorists and wants to deny people of that religion entry to the country, and who mocks and denigrates women, minorities, and other fellow citizens. He claims to be "taking citizenship seriously." By that, he means "America first."[1] His campaign and his election have been met with outrage by those with a different vision of how citizens of a diverse country should act in relation to each other and how they should act toward other people who seek work, freedom, or refuge in their country. Divergent views of citizenship are clashing.

A closed-in view of citizenship in the United States, Europe, or any other political entity confronts the reality of human mobility and the variety of forms of community and affinity that people experience, whether in new homes or places their ancestors have lived in for generations. Mobility and multiple forms of belonging are not new phenomena. But only in the past half century, with the collapse of colonial empires that relegated most inhabitants of the territories they controlled to the status of subject, did people around the world begin to assume that every human being was—or should be—a citizen somewhere.[2]

As political leaders and intellectuals came to imagine a world in which all people would have the rights of citizens within their own states, they were also thinking of a world in which people shared in norms of human progress and efforts to end poverty and injustice. Parts of these goals have been realized in certain times and in certain places, but justice and equality remain elusive objectives, both within and among states. Some collectivities that regard themselves as a "people" if not a "nation"—Palestinians, Kurds, Roma, Rohingya—have found no place in the global system of states; others confront states that assert their indivisible sovereignty with claims for recognition. Meanwhile, thousands of Africans risk their lives in rickety boats to get to Spain or Sicily in the hope of entering the bottom tier of the European job market and thousands of Syrians flee for their lives from their own country—reminders that the making of a world of citizens has not produced a world of equals or a world of justice.

Injustice and inequality cannot be contained within borders. The large-scale influx of immigrants into Europe produces tensions and scapegoating that leaders of xenophobic political parties exploit to gain support among "native-born" French, Dutch, Danish, or German citizens who feel themselves excluded from economic opportunities. Exclusion *within* European countries is as much an issue as walls being erected around the continent.

Inequality in Europe and the Americas has become so extreme that some observers worry that social bonds built up over many decades are eroding. Pierre Rosanvallon, a specialist on European social and political history from the eighteenth century to the present, points to the "silent decomposition of social ties and, simultaneously, of solidarity" and notes that "inequalities have never before been so widely discussed while so little was being done to reduce them."[3] People now feel incapable of acting as citizens as they once did in making European countries more socially just.

We live in a world that is diverse, unequal, and connected. It is unclear whether the fiction of a global order that assigns each individual to citizenship within a territorially defined state provides a stable basis for world order or corresponds to the reality that millions of people live.[4] It is even less clear that values that many of us attach to humanity as a whole can be honored when their enforcement is relegated to states that lack the will to enforce them nationally or to agree upon institutions to do so globally.[5]

Nonetheless, millions of people are defending their rights as citizens against governments that threaten to take them away or foreigners who threaten to dilute them, and others seek citizenship in the states in which they are seen as foreigners. Citizenship is both a powerful and an ambiguous concept, ambiguous not least in relation to territory. Mobile people identify with different locations at the same time; they might have legally defined rights in places other than that in which their citizenship is located—rights to welfare, education, sometimes even to vote in local elections.[6]

Whether states exclude potential new citizens or seek them to augment their labor force or to respond to humanitarian imperatives, they are engaged in intense debates over what threshold of commonality is required to allow immigrants to accede to the status of citizen.[7] The specifics of these tensions are new; the existence of such complexities is not.

This book focuses on citizenship as a divisible and flexible bundle of rights and obligations in relation to a political entity. Running through the discussion of citizenship in many times and places in the following chapters are two central themes. First, I will bring out the varied kinds of political units in which citizenship could be exercised and contested, including cities, empires, federations, and culturally defined communities as well as nation-states. Second, I will suggest that citizenship has not simply been a common status that presumes and perpetuates the equivalence of citizens, but a framework for debate and struggle over the relationship of political belonging to religious, linguistic, and cultural difference and over the tensions between the citizenship ideal and political oligarchy and economic inequality.[8]

Citizenship entails belonging to some sort of political collectivity. It is a different type of relationship than that of a follower to a leader, be it a lineage elder, a chief, a noble, or a king. We could characterize these personal relationships as "vertical," while citizenship—as membership in a political entity—is "horizontal." Citizens exist in relation not just to a leader or in a more abstract sense to a state, but to each other. This distinction in ideal types is further complicated by each historical situation. Citizens are not only connected horizontally to their fellow citizens, but vertically to people with more or less wealth, power, or influence than they have. The degrees to which these different sorts of attachment play out vary greatly.

The study of citizenship confronts a tension between a "minimalist" definition of citizenship as "an 'institution' mediating rights between the subjects of politics and the polity to which these subjects belong"[9]—and a maximalist definition that insists that citizenship necessarily entails the rule of law, full participation in making political decisions, equality among all citizens, and a list of rights such as free speech and the protection of private property—in short, the premises of liberal democracy. The latter is a normative and historically specific conception, often dated to the French Declaration of the Rights of Man and of the Citizen of 1789, or more generally to the breakthroughs in political thought in western Europe in the eighteenth century.[10] To assert that citizenship *should* entail a set list of rights is to make an argument. To *define* citizenship based on such a list of rights or the sovereignty of the "people" is to narrow the domain of inquiry and to begin with an answer rather than to pose the most critical question: what is the relationship between the fact of "belonging" to a political unit and the possibility of making *claims* on that unit and those who govern it?[11]

That the rulers of some polities regarded citizenship in an exclusionary way, insisting that some people who owed obedience to the state were citizens while others were not, makes clear that the definition of citizenship is itself in certain historical situations the object of struggle. Instead of starting out with too categorical a distinction between the "citizen" as bearer of rights and the "subject" as rightless member of a political unit, we can explore the grey area in which people struggled over what it meant to be part of a polity.[12]

Might not horizontal relationships—of citizens with each other—put pressure on vertical ones? Might not people who do not benefit from a powerful patron find common cause with people like themselves against the exclusions from which they suffer? If a state is to sustain the allegiance of its citizens, is it in some degree constrained to provide them security or perhaps mechanisms to insure order, if not improvement, in their lives? When ruling elites concede something to "their" people, might that not that encourage them to take for granted a certain status and possibly to ask for more? Might citizenship be contagious, as people see examples of something to gain by attachment and loyalty to a polity? By leaving open the relationship of belonging and rights—and of horizontal and vertical relationships—one can study citizenship beyond the limited context of post-1789 Europe and its extensions, and also understand more of the dynamics of claim-making in Europe itself and the range of political possibilities that process has opened up, and sometimes shut down. Citizenship has a much longer history than the nation-state. The lineage of the concept in Europe and its offshoots dates to the Greek city-state and the Roman Empire. It implied membership in a political community and expectations that the unit and its leaders would provide protection against outsiders and judicial institutions to regulate relations among members. Its implications for participation in political decisions, however, was variable and often contested. Both the vocabulary with which citizenship was conceptualized and the debates over its significance have inflected considerations of citizenship ever since. The Romans, unlike the Greek city-states, saw the possible offer of citizenship as a way of attaching conquered people to the expanding empire. To some historians of the Roman Empire, no other polity, before or since, "has been so grand that it could claim to encompass the whole world or attempt to create a form of universal citizenship that was open to all comers."[13] Yet the possibilities of inclusive citizenship have kept coming back.

When, in the aftermath of France's defeat in World War II, an assembly was elected to write a new constitution for a new French republic, its members debated whether to continue the practice of the previous century to limit citizenship rights to the population of European France and select portions of its overseas territories or to give a renewed legitimacy to France's empire by extending those rights to all inhabitants of French territories in Asia, Africa, and the Pacific. Several participants in these debates evoked the edict of the Roman emperor Caracalla, who in AD 212 extended Roman citizenship to all free and male inhabitants of the empire. For one side in the debate, imperial citizenship—and this phrase was used—would mark

France as an inclusive, grand power, acknowledging the ultimate equality of all peoples within its embrace without demanding that they give up what some called their "local civilizations." Their opponents mocked the idea of a new edict of Caracalla, a seemingly anachronistic and pretentious assertion in a world in which distinctions of power, culture, and race were fundamental and, they insisted, legitimate. The advocates of the 1946 edict of Caracalla prevailed, and the constitution of the postwar French Republic proclaimed that the inhabitants of its overseas territories had the rights of the citizen. Rome's template for citizenship as inclusion in empire and France's understanding of citizenship as the sovereignty of the "people" were linked in a way that a conventionally national perspective on history obscures.

Imperial citizenship was a concept that could capture the political imagination of Africans and Europeans in the mid-twentieth century.[14] Empires, incorporating diverse populations by violence and other methods, had long been a fundamental unit of political membership. Empires were both incorporative and unequal. In the postwar years, political leaders like those of French West Africa explored alternatives such as federations that would remain incorporative and diverse but would become more equal. Other people saw themselves as members of collectivities—as Arabs, Jews, Blacks, Slavs, etcetera—dispersed around the globe with different relations to specific territories. In the end, decolonization ended up in the creation of nation-states; the number of political units in the world went from around 50 in 1945 to nearly 200 today. The division of the world's people into distinct citizenries came in the last half century to be considered so normal that alternative conceptions passed for a time out of view.

Whether people's rights of speech and protection against arbitrary authority would be protected or whether they would have a chance to have a decent standard of living or the social protections that were coming to be expected in Europe and North America depended on whether the individual states actually worked for their citizens. In much of the world this has manifestly not been the case. Hence, activists and scholars have had to confront the question of where rights and citizenship can and should be located. Citizenship in a nation-state, in itself, neither guaranteed the protection of people's rights nor assured a satisfying response to the complexity of people's sense of belonging.[15]

Multicultural, Flexible, Global, and Other Citizenships

In looking beyond national identification, scholars and activists have introduced such concepts as multicultural citizenship, multinational citizenship, multilevel citizenship, diasporic citizenship, flexible citizenship, and global citizenship.[16] Citizenship is proving to be a capacious concept, allowing us to think about forms of belonging and their relationship to states in a variety of ways and to address the old and new problems of people living both within and beyond territorial boundaries and of states that both protect and abuse their citizens.

There is a danger from this proliferation of adjectives: the noun may become too diffuse to be useful.[17] It is also important to recognize that, in any historical situation, people do not necessarily act in accordance with clearly defined categories. Those categories are themselves changing as people make claims, as they devise institutional mechanisms for determining who belongs in a polity, what if any rights and obligations their membership will entail, and the relationship between the territorial fixity of political units and the way people move about. We need to balance the need for definitional precision against the need to analyze the terms in which people understand ambiguous and changing situations.

Some observers see a "European citizenship" that already exists in law—built upon citizenship in a Member State (France, Germany, Italy, etcetera) of the European Union—as a harbinger of a citizenship that is both portable and divisible, so that, for instance, people have rights to social benefits in one country and vote in another. But social and political protections remain fragmented and under threat, and whether European citizenship can capture the political imagination of the people who bear it is uncertain.[18]

Citizenship is the right to have rights—or, better, the right to *claim* rights.[19] It is the right to claim rights somewhere, as members of some kind of political unit. Citizenship rights differ from human rights, which—whatever they entail and however they might be enforced—attach in theory to the entire species and the entire earth. While citizenship is not a tightly bounded notion, it is most useful when instead of encompassing any kind of political activity or any notion of belonging it focuses on relationships of individuals and collectivities to formal political institutions.[20]

T. H. Marshall's famous theory of citizenship distinguished three levels—civil, political, and social—arranged sequentially, defining citizenship as protection of the person, as participation in politics, and as a claim on at least a minimum level of collective resources. Margaret Somers questions the hierarchy, insisting that the social—the existence of people in relation to each other and to collective resources—is not an outgrowth of civil-political citizenship but a basic part of the human condition. Citizenship recognizes and gives substance to "attachments and inclusion" among people.[21] She points to a tension that is fundamental to debates over citizenship: between citizenship as a recognition of the rights-bearing person, engaging in markets and political arenas as an individual protected from an overbearing state, and citizenship as a social construct, based on relationships in which the social body as a whole is protective of material welfare and a sense of commonality. People can be attached to different political communities at the same time. Today, one of those attachments—actual or desired—is almost always citizenship of a state. What is less clear in the past and present is the relationship of citizenship in a state to the other forms of belonging that are important to people's existence.[22] In some places, the state might be remote—although rarely absent—and other forms of community more salient.

Some scholars of Africa think the concept of citizenship effectively describes the sense of belonging and modes of political participation in the institutions and cultural practices of particular ethnic groups to which people may feel more attachment than they do to an internationally recognized state. Scholars of migration think that the combination of ties to countries of emigration, rights acquired in countries of immigration, and networks established within the migratory pattern constitute, for at least a portion of the people in motion, a kind of "flexible citizenship."[23] Many migrants, however, lack the right papers to move about. Trying to enter a country other than their own, they face barriers that are formally based on their nationality but also reflect distinctions of race or religion. They are experiencing inflexible citizenship.[24]

Looking at the case of Eritreans who have left their impoverished and conflict-ridden African homeland for Europe or North America, Victoria Bernal shows how closely connected, via the internet and associations, these migrants remain to Eritrea while acquiring citizenship elsewhere: "Eritreans in diaspora," she writes, "are to some degree quasi-citizens in their new homes where they often remain outsiders even if legal citizens, and quasi-citizens of Eritrea where they do not live and whose passport they do not hold, yet where they are recognized as nationals and where they see themselves and are seen as stakeholders."[25]

These notions of flexible, portable, or divisible citizenship address the ambiguities of people's locatedness and sense of belonging in contemporary society. By looking beyond a rigid relationship of individual to state, these concepts constitute a response to postcolonial or postmodern critiques of the citizenship concept itself. Such critiques suggest that conventional notions of citizenship force a rich variety of political associations and ideas into the bounds of state structures, especially those associated with European dominance or European claims that its ways represent universal political principles.[26] Indeed, some defenders of "western" ways of politics insist that conformity to European norms is the only acceptable future for once-colonized people, or they assert that immigrants coming to Europe with their own norms and values are incapable of acting as citizens. Neither the critique nor the defense of a conception of citizenship centered on a simplified view of European political theories gets at the dynamics of citizenship in the context of the rise and decline of empires and of long-distance migration.

As soon as people in the Americas, Africa, and Asia claimed citizenship for themselves, the concept took on different meanings. People of diverse origins across large spaces could claim recognition as "imperial citizens" with all the attendant rights; they could seek recognition as a "nation" spread over different continents; they could seek to constitute new states; they could advocate forms of citizenship that were inclusive, exclusive, or something in between. The following chapters will discuss debates over such possibilities, including the attempt in 1812 to write a constitution setting out the rights of citizens and embracing both Iberian Spain and Spanish America and the insistence of South Asian intellectuals in the nineteenth century that they were citizens of the British Empire (both discussed in chapter 2), as well as the claims of Africans to French citizenship in the 1940s and 1950s (chapter 3). Citizenship does not and cannot preclude other forms of association and mobilization. People live with "multiple, overlapping, and proliferating forms of connectedness and dependency."[27] We should take into account the range of possibilities for asserting political belonging, but as long as states are a political reality—and claims of their outdatedness are themselves outdated—the question is how other forms of affinity articulate with citizenship claims.

Becoming Citizens

Citizenship, as a political concept, offers a dynamic possibility more open than that presented by religion, ethnicity, or kinship, that of *becoming* a citizen. As T. K. Oommen puts it,

> We need the concept of citizenship precisely because it is different from nationality and ethnicity. Citizenship provides the non-national ethnic and minority populations in a multi-national state with a sense of belonging and security. It is a partial compensation for their remaining within the state in spite of their different identity from the mainstream, dominant nation or nationalities.

What Oommen refers to, somewhat awkwardly, as "citizenization" implies both that individuals can adapt to the political culture of the society in which they seek to be members and that the political culture can adapt to the diversity of its constituents.[28] These processes are often the objects of struggle. Citizenship certainly excludes, but debate over the criteria of inclusion is internal to the construct. A major question is whether it is limited to people of a certain religion or other particularistic attribute or focused on people's adherence to a political unit. Some commentators term the former conception of citizenship "ethnic," the latter "civic."[29]

The high stakes of inclusion are why rules for the acquisition of citizenship are often contested. Most polities want to reproduce their citizenry: they accept that citizenship is transmitted by birth, either by the fact of birth occurring on the state's territory—*jus soli*—or by virtue of descent from a recognized citizen, regardless of whether the individual was born on the territory of the state—*jus sanguinis*—or more typically by some combination of the two.[30] Critics worry that *jus soli* awards citizenship to people with no more than an accidental attachment to the social and cultural arrangements of the country. Others worry that *jus sanguinis* makes it difficult to integrate long-resident migrants and that it reifies an ethnonational community—a community of blood—defined against outsiders.[31] Whether born or naturalized, citizens can be the object of efforts at education and acculturation—to teach them the proper way to be the citizen of a particular country.[32]

More difficult still is the question of how high the barrier to foreigners entering the polity should be, given labor needs, humanitarian concerns, and desires to maintain a coherent political community. Naturalization rules might require a long period (5–10 years) of legal residence before granting citizenship. Administrators are likely to be interested in income, police records, language acquisition, degree of cultural assimilation, and expressions of loyalty. Not all members of the host society will be enthusiastic about granting citizenship. The newcomers' cultural patterns might seem alien; they might bring in dangerous ideas or practices; they take jobs; they strain welfare and educational facilities. Controversies abound—in Africa as well as Europe and North America—over setting immigrants on a road to citizenship, keeping them in a marginal status so they can be sent away when no longer useful, or preventing them from entering in the first place. Some of the more thoughtful participants in discussions of these issues stress the importance of avoiding dichotomous thinking: too sharp a distinction between the rights of the citizen and of the resident foreigner, too laissez-faire or too restrictive an approach to mobility, too strong or too weak requirements for cultural assimilation.[33]

The discourse of elites and ordinary people is often laden with images of what the proper citizen looks like, what his or her religious beliefs should be, how he or she should behave. The controversies in France over the vestimentary practices of Muslim women—at school or on the beach—reveal a brittleness in the self-representations of a society that proclaims with insistence its attachment to the equality of all citizens of the republic but has trouble with people who want to be citizens in different ways. Insistence on homogeneity and acceptance of difference are both *arguments*; neither is an essence of what citizenship inherently is.[34]

The point is not to try—a hopeless task—to resolve such tensions in one direction or another, but to work with them and to think through the possibilities and constraints in lives that are spatially located but not contained. A state that aspires to an inclusive and democratic future needs to take account of its own diversity and what immigrants, refugees, and asylum seekers bring to it without abandoning all notions of collective control over the process of admitting and integrating new citizens. It has to balance commonality and social complexity.[35] That is the opposite of what many states today are doing.

Recognizing Difference

For theorists like Will Kymlicka and Charles Taylor the cultural dimensions of citizenship need to be given explicit recognition in law and political practice. They start off from the premise that most states, whatever their fictions of commonality, are in fact heterogeneous. Kymlicka and Taylor move beyond the material and judicial implications of citizenship to assert that humans have historically defined themselves by their relationships with each other, creating self-identifying collectivities. Those collectivities are now nested within nation-states. The liberal notion of individual rights, the argument goes, is inadequate to protect collectivities, for without the means to defend language and cultural practices of the collectivity, there will no longer be a common culture in which an individual can participate if he or she so desires.[36] What Kymlicka considers "national cultures" within a polity—he is less sympathetic to immigrant cultures—should have a measure of political autonomy, the right to teach and use their own language, and other rights as a collectivity. The key question is recognition: the state itself should acknowledge the importance of different forms of collective identification among its citizens.[37]

Characteristic liberal arguments have been deployed against such proposals. The most basic is that the very argument that Kymlicka and Taylor make—that the nation-state is a constructed entity that doesn't fully embrace the forms of identification of people within it—applies to groups *within* the state as well. The idea of a homogeneous ethnic group is as much a fiction as the idea of the homogeneous nation-state.[38] Africanist scholars have long stressed that ethnic groups are imagined communities, forged not by the timeless experience of living together, but by the back-and-forth movement of people

in the distant or recent past, by forced incorporation into con-
quering empires or the breakup of such polities, and by the
acquisition of clients or (in the past) slaves.[39] Kymlicka is well
aware that ethnic groups can be patriarchal and oppressive,
and he doesn't want to deny individuals an exit option, but he
is still willing to give groups the power to police their borders
and fix in time their cultural contents. In asserting "that national minorities have societal cultures, and immigrant groups
do not,"[40] he denies the very processes that shape culture in
the context of the movement of people.

By making "recognition" the issue, Taylor and Kymlicka say
little about the social and economic dimensions of citizenship.
States have been instruments for the accumulation of wealth
by dominant classes and they have been instruments for the
protection of people from the consequences of accumulation.
The question of who has voice in deciding how a state will act
and who is entitled to assistance or protection shapes the significance of citizenship. Here the boundary question is crucial,
for capital, commodities, and people move unevenly, seeking
markets, investment opportunities, jobs, land, and protection
beyond borders.

Group rights are not simply a possibility imagined by political theorists; they have existed and exist in practice. The Ottoman Empire, tsarist Russia, and the USSR allocated different
sets of rights to ethnic, religious, or class categories, and "group-
differentiated citizenship" has been a part of the Indian political regime, before and after independence. "Scheduled tribes"
and "scheduled castes" are recognized by the Indian state as
bounded collectivities, with a right to protect their language
and culture, and, in the case of those defined as "backward,"
with special quotas in job allocations and other specific social
benefits (see chapter 3).

On the other end of the spectrum lies the Jacobin version of citizenship, allegedly rooted in the French Revolution's abolition of the division of society into estates (clergy, nobility, third estate), now interpreted to mean that the state cannot recognize social distinctions among citizens.[41] Official statistical agencies in France are not even allowed to collect census data on race or ethnicity, for fear that acknowledging such categories would create their own reality. This conceit doesn't make it easier to study the important place of distinction-making in the history of post-revolutionary France.

Both group-differentiated citizenship and Jacobin citizenship are problematic notions, each in its own way. That the Indian state sees recognition of social entities within it as a means of negotiating modes of participation in a differentiated polity has arguably contributed to its endurance as a democratic polity, but it also encourages groups to look inward, to emphasize their separation from others, to practice the politics of ethnic patronage.[42] In February 2016, members of the Jat—considered a relatively "high caste" group—engaged in violent protest, sabotaging part of the water supply to Delhi, to object to job quotas that favored other castes. Leaders even demanded to be reclassified as a "backward caste" to obtain, in effect, affirmative action as a collectivity.[43] In France, what elites think of as "universalism" appears to much of its Muslim minority as a rigid Frenchness that marks them as alien, dangerous, and excludable. If at first glance a radical defense of egalitarianism and community, the singularity of Jacobin citizenship leaves a significant part of the nation feeling less than equal and less than included.[44] We are left with the question of whether we can think about diversity and inclusion in ways that avoid essentializing the "group" or reifying the "nation."

Although states have long been concerned with policing their borders and communities have worried about burdens that might be placed on them, the stakes rose with the slow extension of welfare states in late-nineteenth and early-twentieth-century Europe.[45] Should those benefits go to citizens? To residents? To workers, whatever their origin? The claim to exclusive—and provable—rights to the benefits provided by a given state gave rise to claims and counterclaims.

The locatedness of citizenship confronted and confronts the apparently "global" dimensions of commerce and finance. That contemporary states are immobile and workers uproot themselves only with difficulty, while capital, technology, and commercial networks are highly mobile, puts pressure on the social benefits of citizenship. Transnational corporations profit as well from international legal mechanisms to enforce "free trade" much stronger than those that sustain social rights, even when such rights have a measure of international recognition under the Universal Declaration of Human Rights of 1948. In turn, threats to what people perceive as their social rights as citizens may give rise to movements to defend a putative national identity, thereby sharpening lines of exclusion.[46] Targeting "immigrants" as the cause of insecurity about jobs and collective identification is a response to today's disjuncture between the mobility of capital and the territorial provision of social rights, but it is not an answer to the underlying problem.

Citizenship is a good concept with which to think about such issues. Because it weaves together citizens' rights and obligations in relation to a political unit, citizenship allows the individual to make claims within the same rhetorical structure as the state asserts its authority.[47] It enables a strong rhetoric of equivalence: the community of citizens should not allow anyone to be a "second-class citizen."[48] For this reason, the stakes are high in deciding who can claim the status of citizen.

Citizenship beyond Borders

People organize within the citizenship construct to claim first-class citizenship, or they want to attach their citizenship to a different political entity, whether by secession or aggression, or they put little value on citizenship in any form and attach themselves to another sort of community—religious, ethnic, or otherwise. People cross frontiers, developing new attachments without necessarily giving up old ones. They might want the warmth or comfort of a natal community or they might seek to escape from patriarchal authority.[49] States can be destructive and oppressive as well as solidaristic, giving rise to collective action to overturn the regime and individual mobility to escape it—an extreme version of which we are witnessing now in flight from Syria or Afghanistan to the European Union.

Some argue that mobility is greater in today's world than in the past and the forms of affinity that are available are more diverse. Yet the location of citizenship has long been open to contestation and complicated by forms of belonging that cut across the membership of all sorts of political entities. People migrate to flee oppression or improve their lives, but they also make claims, individually and collectively, on states for protection and, in recent times, for social benefits, education, and support for cultural expression. At the same time, states may support economic and military initiatives across borders, but they depend on citizens for revenue and labor. They maintain surveillance over citizens and at times impose social norms on them. In both senses, the citizenship construct, in past and present, supplies a measure of fixity to people whose social location is uncertain and whose physical location is variable.

In medieval Europe, a person might be the citizen of a city, but he or she was also subject of a king and hence belonged to a political unit that was to varying extents territorial and patrimonial—combining control of territory with relations based on the personal dependence of followers on the leader. The African living in a kingdom might be a member of a kinship group, under the leadership of lineage elders, but was also subject of a king, by whom he or she expected to be treated according to certain norms and to whom he owed certain obligations. In 1948, the Canadian citizen acquired citizenship of "the United Kingdom and Colonies"; in 1993 the French citizen automatically became a citizen of the European Union. Now many people possess dual citizenship. Willem Maas can thus conclude that "unitary citizenship is the historical exception; more common are varieties of multilevel citizenship."[50]

Different relationships of belonging and space both persist and evolve over time. The first Islamic caliphate of the seventh century tried to define a community of Muslims—the *umma*—that superseded kinship and tribal ties, but as it expanded the caliphate had to recognize the legitimate place of non-Muslims within the polity, a range of social relations that brought converts and clients into the *umma*, and the increasing number of Muslims around the world who did not live under the caliphate's political control.[51] Later on, the Ottoman Empire put together a political field that was both Islamic and multiconfessional; one could be "Ottoman" in different and changing ways, and at the same time be Palestinian or Jewish or Egyptian. By the nineteenth century, the Ottoman Empire was facing the question of whether its complex notions of belonging could sustain the integrity of the empire or whether a more singular notion of an "Ottoman citizenship" would help meet the challenges of the new era.[52] More recently still, certain movements among Muslims reasserted aspirations for a deterritorialized Muslim polity, looking back to the early caliphates and to the *umma*, denying the relevance of citizenship altogether.

Political movements take place not only within boundaries of social and cultural identification, but across them, highlighting the ambiguous and changeable relationship of community, state, and space. When political activists in Great Britain and the United States attacked the slave trade and slavery in the early nineteenth century, they made an issue of the fate of people from an alien continent—Africa—living on plantations in places that most citizens of those countries had never seen. Was the status of the slave on a sugar plantation in Jamaica or a cotton plantation in Alabama a concern because he or she "belonged" in the British Empire or an American state, or because of the slave's humanity? Did subsequent critiques of the inhumane treatment of colonial subjects in one's own empire refer to an implicit imperial citizenship or to an implicit world citizenship—an assertion that everyone should have the right to have rights? Did the worldwide revulsion against the Nazi genocide, the growing consensus in the 1950s that imperial powers should not rule over different peoples, or the growing importance among international organizations from the 1970s of "human rights" push politics beyond the realm of citizenship or suggest that there was another, all-inclusive, level at which the rights generally associated with citizenship deserved protection? Could international tribunals or even the capacity of organizations to publicly shame violators of rights provide instances, more or less effectual, for defending those rights?

When people assert their rights as citizens of a state they regard as theirs, they implicitly acknowledge that other people in other places will be making similar claims, and they raise the possibility that the specific rights they claim should have significance beyond their own political unit. It is nonetheless a big a leap from such an observation to positing the existence of a "global citizenship"; neither a consensus on what such a citizenship should entail nor effective institutions to enforce such a set of norms exist. But citizenship talk is not easily containerized, and the relationship between rights located in a state and universal rights is a dynamic one.[53] Some scholars consider multilevel or flexible citizenship to be "post-national," but as we have seen these constructs are not, in the chronological sense, particularly "post."[54] Claims to rights have long been made in the context of empire or in the name of an all-inclusive humanity. And some intellectuals and activists worry, with good reason, that the prevalence in recent decades of human rights discourse—positing an abstract human and a set of universal rights—reflects not so much a heightened sensibility toward common humanity as the decreasing ability of citizens to undertake political action within state institutions and of class-based organizations, notably trade unions, to defend social entitlements. The individual whose "human" rights are being protected resembles the individual who is a seemingly autonomous actor in the market and the voting booth.[55] This tension between the abstraction of rights and their concrete manifestation has long been fundamental to the politics of citizenship.[56]

To think about citizenship implies that there is also a domain of noncitizenship. Within territorial conceptions today, the distinction between citizens and foreigners is apparently straightforward. In empires, from the reign of Caracalla to the British Commonwealth, not everyone was incorporated on the same terms. Slaves and women—together constituting the large majority of the population—were left out of post-212 Roman citizenship. Imperial regimes have at times insisted that groups within the empire possessed distinct sets of rights (the Russian model) or else distinguished between inhabitants who were "citizens" with all the attendant rights and duties and those who were "subjects," under the empire's jurisdiction but without the status or the rights of the citizen (the nineteenth-century French model).[57]

The distinction between citizen and subject in the French and other empires was not a given characteristic of empire, but was contested over many years. Whether the Declaration of the Rights of Man and of the Citizen of 1789 applied to a culturally, territorially, and politically defined French nation in Europe or to a French empire that included Caribbean islands populated by white planters, mixed-race property owners, and slaves of African origin quickly became the object of debate and violent struggle (chapter 2). The very insistence in revolutionary discourse that no status markings could separate French citizens from each other raised the stakes in the conflict. In seeing how the apparent universality of rights was in practice constricted, some scholars refer to an "anthropological" limitation on citizenship—a certain cultural and social minimum that had to be met to be a citizen.[58]

Hence the argument that certain people could be considered "French" but not citizens, that slaves could be deprived of rights and women could have some rights but not the right to vote, since slaves were dependent on masters and women on husbands or fathers. It was only in 1944 that French women received the right to vote and only in 1946 that the distinction between subject and citizen in overseas France was abolished.

We should avoid the temptation to let a simplified and normative version of the citizenship discourse of France in 1789 stand in for the essence of what citizenship is. Even within western Europe, the notion of citizenship is not uniform. It is less salient in Britain than in France, although the notion of a "freeborn Englishman" carried something of the same valence for subjects of the king or queen as did citizenship for post-1789 France. Rogers Brubaker's pioneering comparative study built on the French and German cases to argue that the laws and politics of citizenship follow different trajectories. While later scholarship suggests that the French-German distinction was not as clear or as stable as he argued, the point remains that citizenship, in both political and legal terms, is a varied and contested phenomenon.[59]

Thickening and Thinning Citizenship

Some specialists who have given much thought to the world-wide significance of citizenship distinguish—and it is obvious which side they're on—between a "thick" and a "thin" citizenship.[60] "Thin" posits a one-to-one relationship of citizen to state that guarantees a fixed set of rights and gives the citizen freedom to participate in his or her individual quality in electoral politics and market relations; "thick" points to the claims of citizens to the material and cultural conditions that sustain their lives. These concepts are not static: some people organize to thicken citizenship, others to thin it out.[61] When pensions are reduced or education made more expensive in the name of austerity, social citizenship becomes a contingent right. When the right to vote is denied as it is in some American states to felons who have already served their sentences or when unemployment benefits are denied because of failure to meet stringent rules, the substance of citizenship becomes conditional, not a quality inherent in the person. Even the most generous welfare states of Europe are accused of treating people not as citizens—as part of a solidaristic political entity—but as "consumers" or "users" of social services, or as "taxpayers" or "producers."[62]

One option we do not realistically have is to ignore the citizenship question altogether. Whether we like it or not, states remain key actors in world politics and they police their borders, provide benefits to at least some of their citizens, and keep others out. We can—and should—talk about citizenship as potentially flexible, divisible, portable, and multilevel rather than as characteristic of a closed political space, but in many states, rich and poor, there are strong pressures coming from part of their citizenry itself to close off that space.[63] We need not be stuck in a dichotomy between a unitary vision of the citizenry of a state and a notion that citizens are divided into distinct self-identifying groups. We can, however, retain an important role that citizenship has played historically—as an "aspiration," an ideal of acting collectively for the common good—even if the basis of the commonality is uncertain.[64]

How much can governments and communities impose their vision of how a person is to act if he or she is to enjoy the full benefits of citizenship? To what extent does the possibility of people *becoming* citizens clash with visions of citizenship as a community of the familiar and the like-minded? Will the multiple affinities that people bring to their relationship with a state or develop over the course of their lifetime enrich or diminish their identification with their fellow citizens? What is the connection between citizens' attachment to their state and the state's ability to meet their expectations—from protection to social benefits? How much inequality is compatible with the notions of belonging inherent in the concept of citizenship? These are among the questions that we, as scholars and as citizens, confront as we face the future—and the past.

CHAPTER ONE

Imperial Citizenship from the Roman Republic to the Edict of Caracalla

WHEN FRENCH POLITICIANS in 1946 evoked the precedent of the decree of AD 212 by the Roman emperor Caracalla extending Roman citizenship to all free and male inhabitants of the empire, they were making clear that citizenship was a relevant concept for an empire, not just for a nation. French legislators knew their classics, although they did not necessarily fully comprehend the import of the edict of Caracalla. We need to look even further back in ancient history to see the persistent debates over citizenship in the context of difference and inequality.[1]

This long history begins with the Greek *polis*, which established a model of citizenship in a city-state that was both democratic and exclusionary. Women were excluded; slaves were excluded; conquest and expansion did not necessarily result in the incorporation of new citizens. The men recognized as citizens, however, were to have a voice in governing its affairs. Greek thinkers were well aware of the tension between a people, moved by emotions as much as by reason, and leaders, motivated by self-aggrandizement as well as by the idea of representing a people. Democracy, autocracy, hierarchy, and oligarchy existed in relation to each other. If the Greek *polis* was spatially circumscribed, it was for some philosophers the only world that mattered—a cosmopolitan setting where people could think of themselves as "citizens of the world."[2]

The Greek word *polis* originally meant citadel, something enclosed. Roman thinkers contrasted the closure of the Greek city-state with what they considered the openness of their own notion of citizenship. Even a Greek philosopher in Roman times could acknowledge that Rome "had made of the whole world a single *polis*."[3] The concept at the core of Roman politics was *civis*, and the word has Indo-European roots connoting family, an outsider admitted into the family, a guest or a friend. "*Civis*," Claude Nicolet writes, "is an associative term: its proper meaning is not 'citizen,' but 'fellow-citizen.'" Romans thought citizenship entailed the melding of people who were of different origins.[4] Citizenship continued to have multiple meanings, in reference to a city, to a wider political community, to the empire as a whole. *Civitas* meant "a polity and a place."[5]

Making Roman Citizens

The transformation of Rome from monarchy to republic (traditionally dated to 509 BC) meant the participation of the free population as a whole in governance through popular assemblies. This did not prevent the emergence of affluent and privileged families and men occupying key roles in day-to-day politics, creating a countercurrent to the egalitarian tendency of republican politics. Under the Republic, Rome undertook expansion into the surrounding region, and its incorporation of conquered peoples gave the city-state its imperial dimension. The region had been occupied by "Latins" organized in a variety of localized polities. Latin initially became an intermediate status between Roman citizen and outsider, but more and more Latins gradually acquired the status of citizen. That gave them a set of rights that were slowly being defined. The right, for example, to serve in the legions of the army—as opposed to the auxiliaries—offered a means of upward mobility. The provinces became increasingly important as suppliers of these citizen-soldiers.[6]

The Republic conferred other rights on its citizens, of which the most important was the right to be tried for a crime or to bring a legal action in a Roman court and to appeal any decision to courts in Rome itself. Emma Dench links Rome's growing power to its incorporative model of citizenship: "The success of Roman imperial ventures depended on the transformation of competing and ethnically diverse peoples of Italy into a Roman war-machine through the transformation of statuses and lands and the enaction of treaties between individual communities and Rome."[7]

Political rights were an essential component of citizenship in the Republic—to vote in assemblies of the people, to stand for office. Expansion necessarily changed the nature of political participation, for an electoral corps of over a million could not fit in the Forum, and not everyone could come to Rome to participate in an assembly. Although assemblies continued to be a part of political life, more and more political action operated through elites, notably senators and magistrates and increasingly military leaders, who in turn called on their partisans for support. Citizenship beyond the city of Rome was exercised within municipalities and provinces as well as through the institutions of the empire. Public opinion was increasingly "parceled in small units," and political relationships became more personal and private. Nevertheless, leaders remained conscious of the dangers of dissatisfaction among the people.[8]

Roman citizenship had a differentiating quality: there were gradations among Romans and among Latins, among the next outward layer of "Italians," and *peregrini*—people who lived within the zone controlled by Rome but lacked citizenship rights.[9] Some communities as a whole were granted "Latin citizenship," and a municipality might achieve a special Roman status. Slowly, Roman rank orders became intertwined with local hierarchies. At the bottom of the emerging rank order came plebeian citizens, the *peregrini*, and on the very bottom, slaves.[10] Craftsmen might be organized in associations of bakers or wine merchants. Women were "not strictly speaking members of the local civic body (*populus*)," but as mothers, wives, daughters, and sisters of the elite played a role in public life.[11]

As Nicolet writes, "the *civitas* was not merely the sum of a number of individuals with equal rights but consisted, properly speaking, of intermediate groups which had to express themselves severally to constitute an expression of the people's will." There were different levels of assemblies and different qualifications in terms of wealth and property for various offices. Magistrates represented the controlling, top-down side of the Roman Republic; tribunes, chosen by a more open, popular assembly, could make the voice of "the people" heard.[12]

As Rome in the late second and early first centuries BC subordinated other states—by violent means or the incentive to cooperate with an increasingly wealthy and powerful entity—the people of those states could acquire the status of *socii* with a restricted set of rights. The position of *socii* entailed tensions in the relationship between Rome and its neighbors and sometime allies. What upset many of the *socii* was not so much that they had lost their independence to Rome, but that they were not fully incorporated into Roman citizenship. Some Romans, like the xenophobic elements in today's Europe, worried that admitting too many Latins to full citizenship rights would encroach on the space for real Romans at meetings, festivals, and games: "Don't you realize they'll take over everything?" opined an opponent of a more inclusive citizenship. The tensions led to the "social war" of 91–88 BC—a bloody conflict between Rome and towns across the Italian peninsula. However mixed the causes of the war, Rome resolved the situation by extending citizenship to all (male) Italians who had fought against Rome and who agreed to lay down their arms. The number of Roman citizens as much as tripled, a decisive step toward the incorporative dynamism of the Roman Empire.[13]

Citizenship did not mean giving up particularity: "the Italians were able, without injury to their local patriotism and particularism, to become members of a new *patria* with an exclusive claim to world domination. They could still be at heart men of Arpinum, Capuans or Gauls from Mantua, while at the same time enjoying a Roman citizenship which did not impose any artificial uniformity."[14] People *became* Roman—in a juridical and political sense—and as people from different places did so, the cultural landscape of the empire became adaptive and varied but was still regarded as Roman. In Gaul during Caesar's time, individuals, not just communities, could follow "routes into the system, while censuses, taxation, and the Roman law that came with Roman citizenship taught new Gauls new ways of behaving."[15]

Citizenship was a defined status, duly recorded. The *census*, under the Republic and afterward, not only counted people, but registered each person's age, sex, parentage, family relations, civil status, domicile, tribal membership, and property. It differentiated the citizenry, and such differentials could determine eligibility for particular offices. The inscription of citizenship and the rituals had a further effect: "As a soldier, a taxpayer or recipient of public bounty, and an elector, the Roman was made to realize at every stage of his life that he was a *civis*, a member of a community that existed because of him and for his benefit."[16] The census was extended, however imperfectly, across the empire, requiring heads of households to present themselves and their family information to magistrates. The census marked both the fact of membership in an imperial polity and the wealth and status differentials within it.[17]

The Roman institution of the "colony"—*colonia civium Romanorum*—gave later generations the word and extended the practice of Greek city-states of implanting people in another's territory. As early as the fifth century BC, Romans were establishing communities of citizens away from the capital. Becoming a colonist could be attractive to less well-off Roman citizens or for others who, while away from the ferment of the imperial center, might find in the colony a place to fulfill their ambitions. Colonists remained attached to their Roman citizenship. The colonies did not acquire, until later, the relative autonomy of municipalities. The colony, however unwelcome initially to the people among whom it was implanted, could show them the attractions of Roman ways of life, the commercial possibilities that imperial linkages provided, and the value of alternatives to local hierarchies. Taken together, the colonies and the outward extension of citizenship meant that Rome's expansion was more than a matter of violent conquest. Peter Garnsey goes as far as to argue, "we can see that the spread of citizenship held the key to the prodigious success of Rome as an imperial state."[18]

Debating Power and Inequality in Republican Rome

In an insightful book, Joy Connolly argues that politics in the Roman Republic should be seen as a framework for debate, and especially debate over status, hierarchy, wealth, and inequality. Her argument points to the antiquity of a perspective seen in scholarship on citizenship today: that citizenship is not simply a relationship of individual to state, not simply a reflection of a bounded community set against those outside, but a framework in which people ponder the structure of society. While citizenship seemed to express the idea of "being" Roman—a horizontal conception of society—Rome was an oligarchical polity and a stratified society. Awareness of that tension, Connolly argues, was intrinsic to political argumentation during the time of republican rule in Rome.

As she points out, it is well known that highly regarded Roman thinkers "took for granted" that they lived in a society that enslaved people, disenfranchised women, made a virtue of combat, and was characterized by economic inequality and the power of the wealthy.[19] But she goes on to argue, "what is lost is Roman writers' attention to the deep contradictions at the core of their own thinking."[20]

Cicero, she asserts, was concerned with the different forms of power. He saw the rivalry between the senatorial elite—the epitome of oligarchic politics—and the people as a permanent feature of politics. In his view, the rights of citizens depended on their ability to defend themselves against that elite. Such conflict should be channeled in nonviolent ways—not least into oratory—but it had to be dealt with. The tribunes—closer to the people than the senators—presented an institutional check on the elite, but Cicero also worried about the extremes to which the populace might go.[21]

Roman historians like Livy pointed to moments when the greed of the wealthy was revealed publicly. Tacitus sought to understand the obscuring effects of autocratic power on people's judgment. Other writers agonized over the corrupting effects of money in politics.[22] Connolly finds in classic texts evidence of different voices, of the inequities of society being observed and confronted—but not necessarily eliminated.[23] Perhaps we can find in this understanding of citizenship in its formative context a direct and useful encounter with the inequalities and antagonisms that lurk behind the equivalence that citizenship has seemingly entailed.

Citizenship under the Emperors

What does it signify, after the Republic had given way to dictatorship and monarchy, that citizenship continued to be extended far and wide and the state still sought to legitimize empire by underscoring conquered people's sense of belonging within it? Did Roman citizenship become transformed from a practice of political engagement to a judicial status that provided protection but little voice, from active to passive membership in a political community?[24]

These are questions that affected the remaining centuries of Roman empire. A durable component of Roman citizenship was the juridical status it conveyed. When, famously, Saint Paul was being prosecuted, he could call out "Civis Romanus sum," I am a Roman citizen. This invocation did not save him from prosecution, but it did save him from the tyranny of the local powers and conveyed to him the right to be heard by a proper Roman court. Citizens took these rights with them wherever they went within the empire.[25] In the histories of many empires, belonging to an imperial community conveyed the possibility of appealing to the emperor or tsar over and above local aristocrats, local patriarchs, and local tyrants.

At the same time, some of the Republic's institutions continued to have influence under the monarchy: the Senate and the popular assemblies, the magistracies, and the priesthoods. The emperor worked with these institutions, and scholars at the time tried to hold onto something of Rome's republican conception of itself.[26] Senators continued to be respected and influential; tribunes conveyed something of popular sentiment. The army became more powerful than ever, and emperors tried to use their own praetorian guard to offset the power of the legions, not always with success. Rome was often torn by intrigue, and both the praetorians and provincial legions could at times be king makers or assassins. But, Greg Rowe insists, emperors "ruled through republican forms." And with the conquests of Britain and parts of the eastern Mediterranean, "Roman citizenship spread" wider still.[27]

Roman citizenship did not mean a uniform, horizontal Romanness covering the entire empire. As Clifford Ando puts it, "placing the governance of cities in the hands of upper-class individuals whose self-interest aligned them with Rome ... held good throughout the empire." The structure of the empire allowed for the development of relationships, between high- and low-ranking people in the provinces, between local oligarchies and Roman officials. Loyalty to the empire was compatible with continued identification with the culture of particular provinces. Cities were allowed to use their own laws. Residents, however, had a variety of legal statuses, and magistrates were not necessarily local; the influence of Roman law grew over time. Roman citizens retained the right of appeal to a Roman court.[28]

The Roman elite was mobile. One could be born, like the emperor Septimus Severus (Caracalla's father), in "Africa" (present-day Libya and Tunisia), in a family of mixed Italian-African origins, make a career in Rome and Africa, marry a woman from Roman Syria, and end up at the top of the political hierarchy. Inscriptions on the graves of ordinary soldiers in one part of the empire reveal their origins in others.[29]

The Edict of Caracalla

This brings us to 212 and the edict of Caracalla, officially known as Constitutio Antoniniana. The emperor and his edict are something of a puzzle for historians, for there is little to go by other than the short text.[30] Caracalla became sole emperor that very year after assassinating his brother Geta, with whom he had shared the throne. Some Roman commentators attributed his edict to the empire's need for more revenue, for citizens paid taxes and aliens did not. Some considered the edict a largely empty gesture. Current scholarship considers the edict an important act, but not a bolt from the blue. The vast but troubled empire was drawing on its long-term strategy of bounded inclusivity, extending rights and the aura of being Roman across its domains. Although most people in Italy already enjoyed citizenship and the colonies and the cooptation of local elites created pockets of citizenship elsewhere, the eastern parts of the empire and rural areas of the western empire were not so blessed. Perhaps two-thirds of the free population of the provinces were not citizens before the edict, so its impact affected a vast number of Romans.[31]

Caracalla was making a dramatic gesture, binding together a huge and complex spatial structure. As Mary Beard writes, "More than 30 million provincials became legally Roman overnight. This was one of the biggest single grants of citizenship—

if not *the* biggest—in the history of the world."[32] Yet by excluding slaves and women from citizenship, Caracalla was not depriving a masculine Roman elite of dependents and labor. Distinctions between different kinds of Roman citizens did not disappear.

What Caracalla's edict did not do was expand citizens' political role: Rome was still ruled by uneasy compromises between oligarchy, autocracy, and lingering republican principles. Citizenship continued to convey the possibility of advancement to the higher orders of a stratified society and, with the right patronage, a chance at becoming a magistrate or a senator, but it was not a recipe for democratic rule. It had all along been a juridical status, and now citizens throughout the empire could come under Roman law governing family and commerce. Since the law had treated property, inheritance, and contracts among citizens and noncitizens differently, the generalization of citizenship simplified legal life across the empire.[33]

Local autonomy—and overlapping jurisdictions between local and Roman courts—meant that citizenship rights continued to be exercised at the level of the city, province, and empire. Status distinctions within the category of citizen persisted. The lower end of the spectrum was a grey area where slaves, manumitted slaves, *peregrini* (including recently arrived migrants), and the poorest citizens did not receive equal justice. The edicts and silences of post-212 Roman law suggest that most acquisitions of citizenship came from liberation from servile status. *Peregrini* did not have to go through a judicial procedure to become citizens because they were now assumed to have that status, and "barbarians" could acquire some of the rights of citizens while retaining their own "citizenship" in a barbarian kingdom or "nation." Citizenship could be taken away, part of a penalty known as *infamia*.[34] These limitations notwithstanding, Caracalla's edict greatly expanded the number of people whose lives were affected by Roman law and in that sense, it, as Nicolet states, "bore within itself the notion of cosmopolis that was almost realized by the Empire" and which it would transmit to the Catholic tradition.[35]

When French legislators in 1946 cited the Edict of Caracalla as a precedent for extending citizenship throughout the French Empire, they were referring not only to the affirmation of belonging to an imperial polity or to the recognition of all inhabitants of the empire as the bearers of certain rights, but to the precedent that the Roman Empire set for the continued place of local traditions and laws in the lives of its people. They went on to discuss how far the French state could go in recognizing within its purview different regimes of personal status, distinct from the French civil code.

But citizenship in twentieth-century France had meanings that were absent from third-century Rome. Since the eighteenth century, the language of equality had become a fundamental, if problematic, part of the notion of French citizenship. In 1944, at long last, French women had obtained the right to vote, and in this respect the concept of universal suffrage now seemed to mean what it said. Over the course of the twentieth century, French people had come to expect that social benefits would accrue to the citizen, but not necessarily to the noncitizen legally or illegally in France. Rome was a hierarchical and oligarchic polity; France was claiming to be egalitarian and democratic. Extending citizenship from the 50 million or so French people who had that status before 1946 to an additional 50 million, living for the most part in relatively impoverished territories in Africa and Asia, presented a political, economic, and social challenge unlike that faced by Caracalla. The leaders of social and political movements in the colonial empires knew the context in which they lived—demands across the globe for an end to exploitation and inequality within and among states—and they posed a powerful challenge to imperial rule as it actually was.

But the Roman comparison that legislators made in 1946 was not inapt and is still of interest 70 years further on. It is not just that Rome gave us much of our vocabulary for discussing politics and governance—including the word "citizen"—but that the tensions intrinsic to the extension of power over space and diverse peoples have occupied some of the best minds of those times and ours.[36] We live in a world in which polities are highly unequal within themselves and in relation to each other. People are connected in ways that they may see as constitutive of their being or constraining their freedom of action. Extremes of violence have attended the putting together of diverse polities, but empire builders then faced the problem of what to do after they had suppressed resistance to their incorporative violence: how to maintain control over large spaces and diverse peoples, who often retained significant political, economic, and cultural resources, from whom cooperation had to be extracted at a bearable cost. All empires needed intermediaries, some sort of vertical connection to extend power from the top downward and outward. Citizenship represented, in the history of world empires, a quite particular—indeed unusual—mechanism to accomplish such ends. Not all imperial rulers possessed the self-confidence of Roman elites in both their coercive and incorporative power.

The interest of Caracalla's edict was not that it set a pattern but that it posed a possibility. Rulers might experiment with different ways of encouraging and shaping institutions and modes of thought that enabled many people to see a place for themselves within a polity, whether that polity was an empire, a federation, a city-state, a kingdom, a chieftaincy, or an assemblage of kinship groups. If we focus not only on the incorporative dimension of Roman citizenship, but on the debates and conflicts that it entailed, we can appreciate another set of possibilities: a long history of debates and conflicts taking place within the politics of citizenship. Today, we can—and indeed we should—discuss the relationship between participation in a community defined by territorial boundaries and civic institutions and belonging to collectivities defined by religion, ethnicity, occupation, race, or gender. We need to see questions of inclusion and diversity in relation not just to the protection of individual rights in a polity but to social structures that can enhance or impede the chances of individuals and families to achieve a decent livelihood and dignity. Roman intellectuals, 2000 years ago, were aware of the tension between citizenship, inequality, and difference. Those tensions remain with us. A long-term view of such conflicts suggests that the goal should not be to come up with a single set of conceptions or practices that will resolve these tensions, but to live with them critically and creatively.

CHAPTER TWO

Citizenship and Empire—
Europe and Beyond

THE VOCABULARY and much of the arguments that shaped discussions of citizenship ever since the Roman Republic did not originate in the context of a nation-state. The story of citizenship begins with empire, and starting with Rome focuses our attention on the relationship of people from different places with different languages, cultural orientations, and social connections to the inclusionary dynamic of citizenship. Moreover, the oligarchical and authoritarian dimensions of Roman history lead us to ask about the degrees of inequality in wealth and power that are compatible with the commonality of citizenship. Citizenship is not just a status, but a construct used to make claims. Hence it is an unstable concept, with the potential to become more inclusionary or exclusionary and to entail shifting configurations of rights and obligations.

The word "citizenship" has European roots, but the question of political belonging is a general one. We can ask about the relationship of the citizenship concept to ways of thinking about political belonging in other parts of the world. The comparative perspective broadens the scope of inquiry, but it only takes us so far, for at a certain point, with the deployment of European power across the world, different political structures came into unequal relationship with each other, and the language of citizenship became a terrain in which claims and counterclaims were made within European empires and within other imperial regimes. When movements in different political and cultural contexts invoked citizenship, it acquired new meanings.

Cities and Citizens

The history that I have been telling focuses on empire, but it takes us to other kinds of units—the city, the province, the nation-in-the-making—and it takes us from the rule of an emperor to the sovereignty of a people. It doesn't quite leave the framework of empire, for the possibility of a polity expanding to include, forcibly or otherwise, diverse people was ever present, and with it the question of their status in relation to the state and the possibility that citizens might want to distinguish themselves from incorporated "others" by the way they looked, the beliefs they held, or the manner in which they lived.

A classic theme in European history and sociology is the citizen as city dweller. The fall of the Western Roman Empire in the fifth century AD put an end to the world-spanning, inclusive, imperial notion of Roman citizenship, giving way to membership—in various forms—in a variety of what the Romans would have called barbarian kingdoms.[1] The most expansive of post-Roman polities in western Europe—notably that of Charlemagne—were neither as durable nor as capable of providing the juridical and political institutions that had preserved the vital role of citizenship in the empire. Relationships of lordship—of lord and vassal, of lord and peasant—predominated in the European countryside amidst attempts at monarchical consolidation. Nonetheless, the vital exchange economy of cities, the importance of social grouping on the basis of skill or economic role, and the role of economically active urbanites in city governance have made the city a locus of citizenship. Both Latin-based and Germanic vocabulary, with the overlap of city and civic, civil, and citizen, Bürger, Bürgerschaft, Staatsbürgerschaft, and hence bourgeois and bourgeoisie—sew city life into the fabric of social categories.[2] Max Weber famously contrasted the dynamism of the European city's associative life to the rest of the world's fixation on clan and tribe, although this argument has been torn apart from both ends.[3]

Citizens of the Kingdoms of Spain

For an alternative perspective, we can look at the way Tamar Herzog locates citizenship in early modern Iberia. What we today call Spain was divided into multiple kingdoms, and in each local magnates—with land and followers—and the elites of cities exercised considerable political influence. In Castile, the largest of the kingdoms, the Cortes (Parliament) in the late fourteenth century insisted that the king appoint to offices only "natives" of the kingdom—not foreign vassals personally loyal to him. But the Cortes did not define native in a clear way. Jurists and political elites relied on a more subjective notion of belonging to a community—a matter of birth and residence, to be sure, but also of integration into local networks, visible loyalty, religious observation, fiscal responsibility, and reputation. Herzog calls this "local citizenship" or *vecindad*. Citizenship, she says, was performed. The native population of Castile, then, was an amalgam of local communities. Each community was defined by the judgment accorded by its established members. Castile remained a distinct kingdom even when, in the late fifteenth century, its queen married the king of Aragon and created a dynastic composite that ended up linking—but not fusing—what became known as the kingdoms of Spain.

The category of "natives of the kingdoms of Spain"—or "Spaniards" for short—was an amalgam of these amalgams, developing in the sixteenth century. Citizenship was a matter of civil law, criteria established by communities, and relations of vassalage and clientage to a monarch.[4]

By then, Spaniards were establishing themselves in the Americas and the kingdoms of Spain were part of a still larger composite ruled by the great Habsburg emperor Charles V and his descendants. What was the place of different peoples within a complex polity, including people from Iberian Spain who had established themselves in the Americas, Indians whose communities were conquered by the Iberian invaders, African slaves, and the descendants of various mixes of the above? Commerce between the Americas and Europe was in principle restricted to natives of the kingdoms of Spain. Indians were both insiders and outsiders within this imperial polity, vassals of the emperor by virtue of conquest, perhaps loyal intermediaries to Spanish authorities or possibly dangerous rebels.[5] Missionaries saw their role as creating not only converts, but vassals, and therefore Spaniards. Just as the status of "native" of a kingdom of Spain passed through villages, towns, and cities, Indians' integration into the empire passed through "their civic membership in a political community," through demonstrative belonging to a locality. Taken together, Indian communities belonged in the Republic of Indians, distinct from the Republic of the Spanish, but movement and mixing blurred the line.[6]

While Indians could be included in the status of Spanish native, the law did not say they were the same kind of citizen.

Mediating citizenship status through local communities provided means for making distinctions. Jurists were careful to insure that land rights did not attach to the communities to which Indians belonged, at least as long as settlers were interested in those lands. So the structures of inequality—indeed of dispossession—were inscribed within a system that was incorporating much of the Indian population as vassals of the king, as potential converts, and as members of a hierarchy of communities with the kingdoms of Spain at the top. In places where Spanish officials could claim that Indians had failed to "improve" their land for agriculture, the appropriation of that land could be justified. Where Indians resisted the power of the crown, there was all the more reason to dispossess them.

Indians were not rightless, but their rights were conditional. When Bartolomé de las Casas raised the question of how Spaniards were violating the norms of Spanish monarchy by their treatment of Indians, he provoked a long debate over what protection they had as humans and as members of a civic order created by empire.[7] Slaves were not a subject of this debate; they were defined as African and as "foreigners," excluded altogether from citizenship.[8] "Natives" of the Spanish Americas, like "natives" of the kingdoms of Spain, had a place *within* the Spanish empire. But not an equal place. Citizenship was not a direct or unmediated relationship of individual to state, nor was it a leveling mechanism. It passed through communities, through degrees of belonging, and through hierarchies of difference.

Citizenship within and beyond Empire: The Cádiz Constitution of 1812 and Its Aftermath

When I presented early versions of my research on citizenship in twentieth-century French Africa to historians with different regional specialties, scholars of Spanish America sometimes

observed that, according to my description, the French constitution of 1946 resembled the Cádiz constitution of 1812. In
both cases, the constitutional framework under debate was
imperial, defining a space of citizenship that spanned oceans,
emerging from colonization but potentially defining an inclusive citizenship for an empire of diverse peoples. In both situations, constitutional debates unleashed anxieties that the citizenship of people who thought of themselves as the most fully
Spanish or French was being diluted by a too-inclusive version
of political community.[9]

The constitution of 1812 emerged from a particular conjuncture in the early nineteenth century: Enlightenment ideas,
inter-empire wars, attempts to preserve or undermine imperial trade monopolies. The elites of Spanish America knew the
French Declaration of the Rights of Man and of the Citizen of
1789 and the American Declaration of Independence of 1776.
Merchants in Spanish American ports were chafing at the restrictions on trade outside of the empire's channels, and they
were alienated by the monarchy's attempts to impose more
central control and higher tax burdens on the Americas. Then,
Napoleon's conquest of Spain in 1808 left royalists in control
(with British help) of only a small patch of territory including
the port city of Cádiz. The American territories and the Philippines now constituted a colonial empire with only the most
marginal of metropoles.

Even as local *juntas* in the American provinces assumed considerable power and as merchant elites in the Spanish Americas tried to diversify their commercial connections against
the monopolistic designs of Spanish ports and as conflicts escalated, some political leaders on both sides of the Atlantic
realized how much their economic well-being depended on
a semblance of imperial control and how important even a
hollowed-out ideology of empire was to them.[10] Between 1810

and 1812, as rebellions in parts of the Americas spread, American and Iberian leaders converged on the Spanish city of Cádiz to try to hammer out a constitutional compromise. Between a fifth and a fourth of the deputies sitting in the Cortes of Cádiz were from the Americas, most of them favoring liberal principles, in regard not only to trade but to recognition of individual political and civil rights within a framework of empire and constitutional monarchy.[11]

As Jeremy Adelman has emphasized, the thesis of a prior development of a national consciousness does not explain the trajectory of the political conflict that eventually led to the secession of Spanish territories in the Americas. Nor does the idea, advanced by Benedict Anderson, of circuits of communication focusing in on vernacular units, since the deputies from the Americas, like those from Peninsular Spain, were engaged in wider intellectual and political circuits, including the thinkers of the French and British enlightenments. The Spanish American revolutions began as a struggle *within* empire—over conflicting visions, affinities, and interests within an intercontinental Spain—and only over time did they become a struggle to get out of empire. The nations that emerged were not what the leaders of the rebellion initially imagined.[12]

The attempt to devise a constitution for this complex political entity ran into conflicts of interest between Peninsular and American Spaniards, but also a conflict over different notions of belonging. The Cádiz constitution of 1812, after difficult compromises, embraced a singular Spanish nation on both sides of the Atlantic. It defined Spaniards as "all free men born and domiciled in Spanish domains and their children, all foreigners with naturalization letters, all foreigners who, without such letters, were citizens of local communities for at least ten years, and all freemen who obtained their liberty in Spain."[13] Spanish America was included on the same basis as any Castilian territory, and Indians were included alongside people whose roots were in European Spain.

From Cádiz emerged a constitutional monarchy, with elections at different levels. Josep Fradera emphasizes the "revolutionary character" of the new political order: "For the first time and at one stroke, hundreds of thousands of Spaniards in the peninsula and across the empire were called to vote and participate in the political process." It was important to recognize Indians as citizens in order to reinforce the authority of the empire over all its lands and peoples. This logic did not apply to Africans and their descendants. The constitution did nothing to bring about the end of slavery. People of mixed African descent would be considered Spanish, but not citizens. They would have no political rights. Africans, unlike Indians, were assumed to be from somewhere else. The exclusion of blacks from citizenship did not reflect a consensus but emerged out of intense debates and concerns about the interests of slave owners, the dangers of slave rebellion, the participation of slaves and ex-slaves on both sides of the independence struggles, and the worries of Iberian Spaniards that too inclusive a version of citizenship would overwhelm their numbers in representative institutions.[14]

The constitution did not recognize linguistic or cultural distinctions in either Iberian or American Spain. The text followed the early Spanish pattern of linking citizenship to an established local community—including an Indian one—or else to service for the state. The lawmakers also refrained from defining within the text what membership in a community actually entailed.[15]

From the vantage point of Iberian Spanish elites, the compromise posed dangers: the inclusion of Indians brought into the domain of citizenship people who were culturally unfamiliar, of uncertain loyalty—and numerous. The issue of representation was crucial, and it was fought over intensely within the Cortes. If Spanish sovereignty was unitary but the composition of the nation was plural, then the weight given to each part of the whole would affect decisions covering the entire empire. If one followed the logic of citizenship and counted each individual, might not the "true" Spanish people of Iberia be outnumbered by people of different categories from the Americas, whose relationships to each other and to Spain were unclear?[16] But there was no consensus in the Cortes on how to balance the recognized components of the Spanish nation; this was a basic problem of "imperial constitutions," in the United States, in revolutionary France, in the Spanish Empire.[17]

The Cádiz constitution abolished seigneurial structures, Indian tribute, and forced labor imposed on Indians (including the system that had been the basis of silver mining). It vested sovereignty in the nation, not in the king, although it gave the monarch the task of implementing the laws. Here we see the delineation of a constitutional monarchy on an imperial scale. The constitution provided for a legal system in which courts operated without regard to individual status, and for elections of representatives at different levels, from municipalities to provinces to the Cortes itself. It mandated a free press. Peninsular and American Spaniards were declared to be equals before the law. But women would not be equal to men; they would not have the vote.[18]

There was strong sentiment from the Americas to fully implement the Cádiz constitution. But when King Ferdinand VII, who had been chased from power by Napoleon, reasserted himself in 1814, he repudiated the constitution. His action escalated the conflict that had already broken out between factions in the Americas who sought autonomy and those who favored monarchy and a close connection to Iberian Spain. As it became clearer that the demands of activists in the Americas would not be met, the dynamic of claim-making within empire turned into mobilization to fight for a liberation whose contours were still undefined. The divide was not quite a war of "nationalists in the colonies" versus "colonial rulers," for the divisions were more complex and volatile than that. The wars of the 1810s were more like civil wars.[19] Elites engaged in combat with each other tried to mobilize support from popular classes and even from slaves and, especially, freed slaves. This effort in turn opened up social questions that were uncomfortable for American elites—just who in a diverse population would be included in the political arena. The revolutionary hero Simón Bolívar was notably wary of popular participation in politics. For him, the nation should be ruled by people with the social and cultural qualifications to do so.[20]

Mobilization for revolution undermined the structures of hierarchical incorporation, but it did not produce the "horizontal" reorganization of society that Benedict Anderson considers the hallmark of the nationalist vision.[21] Slavery remained both a practice and a subject of contention for decades. On the mainland of South America the intensity of the wars for independence and the mobilization by both sides of slaves and ex-slaves all but doomed the continued practice of slavery, although not discrimination against ex-slaves or prejudice against Indians or people of mixed origins in both rural and urban areas. In Cuba, however, where the economy was dependent on slave labor, the planter elite did not rebel, for it needed the protection of the Spanish state. In fact, slavery in Cuba greatly expanded in the early nineteenth century. Only later in the century would the issues of Cuba's colonial status and slavery lead to violent conflict.[22]

Schemes to create federal structures to keep together at least some of the Spanish territories in the Americas did not come to fruition, and the various armies and the political factions that had emerged to fight the enfeebled armies of the Spanish monarchy ended up producing territorially bounded nation-states that were a far cry from what most political leaders, pro- or anti-empire, had imagined ten years before. The imperial citizenship that the constitution had promised in 1812 broke up into an array of territorial citizenships—a pattern that we shall see again in French Africa over a century later. After considerable uncertainty and conflict, all the independent states constituted by the mid-1820s some form of republican regime.[23]

The Cádiz constitution had focused public debate around such concepts as national sovereignty, liberty, equality, division of powers, and constitutional monarchy. Long after Spain had lost its grip on the Americas, these concepts would continue to influence debates on citizen participation in politics, on possible forms of federalism to give recognition to provinces within states, and above all on the importance of constitutional law.[24] With the advent of the territorial states of the Spanish-speaking Americas, struggles for inclusion and equality would be conducted within the construct of national citizenship.

The post-independence decades witnessed efforts to pry open the door of inclusion. Free blacks and mixed-race people, who had been excluded from citizenship, petitioned to acquire the rights of the citizen based on military service or other merit. At the same time, elites endeavored to narrow the political participation of citizens, fearing popular demands that could compromise their economic interests. In parts of former Spanish America, literacy and property restrictions excluded citizens from political participation even as status distinctions were denied recognition in constitutional law. Women and dependent males—including servants and soldiers—were denied the vote in much of nineteenth-century Latin America.[25] In Colombia, writes James Sanders, people on the bottom of the social spectrum "voted, argued, marched, petitioned, struck, boycotted, chastised, assaulted, fought, and died. By doing so, they completely altered Colombia's political culture." They also, at times, acted in *relation* to elites, as supporters, clients, and allies to rival political figures. Other studies have found that people acted politically less as autonomous individuals facing a national state than as citizens of towns and villages, themselves hierarchically organized. Rather than engage actively in politics, some people sought to find a niche in the social structure where they could escape the constraints of the power of landlords, officials, and priests. For Indians, liberal politics could be a two-edged sword, implying recognition as equal citizens, but loss of some of the protections that communities had afforded, especially rights to communal land.[26]

What long-term impact did the constitution of Cádiz have? A lasting one, concludes Hilda Sabato, particularly in making the citizenry, via elections, the ultimate arbiter of political legitimacy. Most countries followed a "zigzag path" toward an inclusive electoral system. The idea that the people should ultimately decide who governed them was fundamental, and participation of popular classes in elections was not necessarily less important than it was in European democracies of the mid-nineteenth century. If formally individualist, citizenship rights in fact were exercised via networks, the development of associations in cities and towns, and patron-client ties, a combination of "horizontal" connections and "strong vertical components" that we shall see elsewhere (chapter 3).[27]

In parts of Spanish America—and Brazil as well—racial mixture became "a sort of official ideology"—an assertion of inclusivity, but also a refusal to recognize the invidious distinction–making that remained a part of social and political life.[28] Electoral democracy, populist authoritarianism, and military dictatorship have all been part of the history of citizenship in

Latin America. Despite efforts of social movements to "thicken" citizenship, "thin citizenship" prevailed in much of Latin America, even when elections were reasonably free. Frances Hagopian points to long-term efforts to forge democratic societies, but laments that many citizens did not participate actively in political life and often ceded public space to demagogic leaders. She adds that "courts, police, and petty bureaucrats mistreated ordinary people in their daily interactions" and people's civil rights were violated by the "hired guns of landowners and drug gangs" who created "their own political rules."[29] By targeting specific portions of the population, such practices not only eroded the specific rights that citizenship conferred, but diminished the very basis of citizenship itself, that is, the right to claim rights. Evalina Dagnino evokes the long-term effect of the extremes of social inequality within Latin American citizenship regimes: "As part of the authoritarian, hierarchical social ordering of Latin American societies, being poor means not only economic, material deprivation but also being subjected to cultural rules that convey a complete lack of recognition of poor people as bearers of rights."[30]

Faced with such limitations in national politics, political movements in twentieth-century Latin America have repeatedly claimed rights in cities and rural areas, and not just in elections but in occupations of land or houses, in demonstrations, in efforts to govern urban neighborhoods in their own way. James Holston terms these actions an "insurgent citizenship" that runs against the "inclusively inegalitarian citizenship" of official circles. Such movements do not seek to disengage with the state; instead they pose demands on it. Mobilization by workers or peasants, villagers or neighborhood residents, counters the exclusionary nature of citizenship by building on the very differentiation of the citizenry. Even during the period of authoritarianism in the 1960s and 1970s in the national politics in Brazil, Argentina, and other Latin American states, urban politics constituted a mode of action when mobilization at the national level was cut off. With the eventual fall of dictatorships, such movements enabled political parties, like the Workers' Party in Brazil, to challenge the control of a narrow elite.[31]

In turn, the efforts of some Latin American regimes to "thicken" social citizenship have been countered both by old elites defending their privileges and by policies in the name of market rigor.[32] Even such moves draw on a rhetoric of citizenship, but its "thin" version, reduced to a "strictly individualistic understanding" in which labor rights and social protections are portrayed as impediments to the free individual acting in a free market.[33]

In discussing citizenship in Spain and Spanish America, I have traced a dynamic, played out over a particular space and time, in which citizenship on imperial, national, and local levels framed political action. Politics, even under constitutional regimes, did not simply imply a direct relation of individual to state, but both drew on and strongly affected social ties— community, clientage, class, race, and different forms of association. Both the vertical and horizontal social ties and the possibility of making claims as a body of citizens—as a people—have shaped the vagaries of politics in nineteenth-, twentieth-, and twenty-first-century Spanish-speaking America.

Claiming Rights: From British Empire to the United States

In British North America, political activists made claims within empire and in the name of imperial political concepts before they brought together a revolutionary movement to exit from empire.[34] The conventional view is that the concept of citizenship is weak in the British case; that citizenship, as such, was not defined until the Nationality Act of 1948, which set out a citizenship of the "United Kingdom and Colonies" (to be discussed in chapter 3).[35] All inhabitants of the dominions, colonies, and metropole had long been subjects of the king or queen. In principle, British subjects were united as "men bound, not to one another, but to a common superior."[36] But they were not rightless.

The English revolutions of the seventeenth century brought forth a notion of parliamentary government, albeit based on a restrictive, property-based franchise. Margaret Somers postulates that the roots of citizenship in Britain are found in the evolution of its judicial system, including the notion of trial by jury.[37] The notion of "the freeborn Englishman" carried weight in the eighteenth century—a strong notion of belonging, which opened up a question of who was entitled to political voice.

What concerns us here are the imperial implications of these political ideas. They did not apply to slaves—who were by the eighteenth century the mainstay of the overseas economy. There was a hitch, however. The famous Somersett case of 1772 ended with a ruling that slavery, while legal in the colonies, had no legal basis in England, a decision that underscored the differentiated nature of law across empire. At the same time, the connections of empire constituted a space in which that differentiation could be debated. Norms in one part of the empire could disrupt other parts. By the late 1780s an anti-slavery movement in Great Britain was arguing that slaves in British territory partook of the Britishness of the territory, and therefore slavery was no more compatible with British justice in Jamaica than in London.[38] The arguments in Parliament over the abuses of the British India Company also made clear that the empire was a moral space. The situation of people in lands most English people had never seen mattered to the integrity of the British polity.[39]

The question of Britishness had powerful implications in another sense. By the 1770s, settlers in North America had become outraged that although freeborn Englishmen, they were not represented in Parliament. Nor did the government allow them to have their own law-making assemblies. They complained too that Indians were themselves making claims in British courts as subjects of the king, and that the Crown was providing insufficient support to settlers in their conflicts with Indian communities.[40] In this context of disagreement over political rights in the space of empire, demands for a distinct citizenship in British North America turned into a revolutionary movement.

It later had to be worked out whether the thirteen colonies would produce thirteen nation-states each with its own citizens or a single, federal state. The vigorous debate over this issue took place among leaders well aware that they lived in a world of empires, and the danger of recolonization by the British or another empire influenced the ultimate decision to create the United States and with it an American citizenry.[41] Citizenship would also have to be defined against Native Americans. Once the states did unite and push westward, the United States defined Indians as distinct "nations" whose separation and subordination were articulated in increasingly harsh ways.[42] Even after the Civil War, the Fourteenth Amendment left "Indians not taxed" out of its rights-bearing purview. To become citizens, Indians had to cease to be Indian—to leave their communities and be assimilated to the dominant culture, in contrast to the provisions of the Spanish constitution of 1812. Only in 1924 did the Native American population of the United States acquire the status and rights of the citizen.

Slaves, through the time of the Civil War, were excluded from citizenship, and free people of color were for the most part either excluded or marginalized from mainstream society and politics. Some of them slowly developed a specifically African American sense of nation. Whether slavery was legitimate in a country that prided itself as free became a question that divided the "white" population.

As early as the 1790s there were divisions among the political elite over how welcoming the United States should be to white immigrants and how much of a place there would be for ethnic particularism, for example for Irish American organizations that claimed to share the values of the Republic that had liberated itself from the British Empire. The naturalization of white immigrants was initially relatively easy, but legislation in 1798 made it more difficult until the political tides turned again and the law on acquiring citizenship became more welcoming for white immigrants.[43]

Changes in laws reveal shifts in attitudes towards inclusion and exclusion of potential new citizens. The Chinese Exclusion Act of 1882 imposed racially based restrictions, and the Immigration Act of 1924 installed quotas based on the number of people from each country of origin recorded in the 1890 census. Both laws aimed at keeping the citizenry of United States predominantly of Northern European roots.[44] The racially based restrictions on Asians were eased in the 1940s and early 1950s, and a new and more open system of immigration enacted in 1965. But the pendulum is still swinging; nativist conceptions of legal and illegal immigration still carry a strong appeal for many Americans. The United States nevertheless has practiced a relatively strong version of *jus soli*, so that someone born on American soil of foreign parents is entitled to citizenship. Despite the vagaries of politics and the frequent lack of clarity of citizenship legislation, citizenship in the United States has remained associated with political rights and equality—for at least some of the people living on its territory.[45]

The formal entry of slaves into the category of citizen after the Civil War reconfigured the politics of racial exclusion, provoking complex and often violent movements to define distinctions and enforce subordination within a regime of constitutional equivalence. Citizenship—as the civil rights movement in the United States well understood—has to be claimed, against others who were deploying their own citizenship rights to deny others.[46]

Subjects and Citizens in the British Empire

Within the remaining British Empire, the question of what kind of polity people belonged to remained complex. As Canada, Australia, and other dominions became increasingly autonomous over the nineteenth century, many of their elites continued to see themselves as part of a British world united by a supposedly common heritage and by whiteness. In the late nineteenth and early twentieth century, the idea of a "Greater Britain" spread across the globe echoed in imperial circles.[47]

However, a large proportion of the subjects of the king or queen of England were not white. When the slaves of the British colonies were freed in the 1830s, they remained British subjects. Some abolitionists and administrators wanted to give property-owning people of color in the Caribbean local voting rights, but their efforts were aborted after a rebellion in Jamaica in 1865.[48] The plantation colonies, set alongside the territories of "white" settlement, present a stark instance of how different parts of empires are governed differently.[49] Giving ex-slaves a voice in Parliament was never a serious question in the British Empire, although, as we shall see, it became one in the French Empire in 1789 and again in 1848. Subjecthood was supposed to convey protection, and when in 1847 a British subject got into a dispute with the Greek government, the Foreign Secretary justified his intervention on the subject's behalf by quoting the famous expression heard under the Roman empire, "*Civis Romanus sum.*"[50]

When the British Empire expanded in Africa in the late nineteenth century, it took in more subjects. Debates quickly broke out over what their Britishness signified—certainly not equality, but perhaps certain protections. The anti-slavery movement took up the cause of liberating African slaves from their indigenous masters where slavery was still practiced "under the British flag," and it campaigned as well against too much use of forced labor by British administrators or settlers. The fact that African subjects were in some sense British gave the humanitarian campaign its rhetoric and lobbying force. British leaders tried to get other colonizing powers to adopt similar norms. They were in effect promoting the international acceptance of the contention that civilized powers should apply some degree of protection to their subjects.

White Britishers were not the only people to make claims on the basis of their place within the empire. Political activists in India began calling for imperial citizenship in the early nineteenth century. There were, of course, many forms and idioms of protest and claim-making that arose in India, as Subaltern Studies scholars have made clear. But the claim for equality, as we have seen in other parts of the world, was coming in the context of empire, not from a "preexisting prototype of nation."[51] Activists interrogated the self-proclaimed norms of their colonizers and demanded an equal place within the political unit into which they had been incorporated. "British imperial citizenship," writes Niraja Gopal Jayal, "was not unlike that of imperial Rome, similarly inclusive in the formal sense, and similarly stratified in reality." As in republican Rome (chapter 1), the British insistence that its subjects were part of a British domain and could not be anything else provided a basis for critique of the excesses and abuses of rulers and a claim to exercise the same rights as those enjoyed by any other British person.[52]

As Britain ceded to its "white" dominions the right to make their own policies, it in effect allowed them to take away from immigrants from other parts of the empire what aspects of imperial citizenship London was willing to concede. In response, the Imperial Indian Citizenship Association was created in Bombay in 1914. It demanded that people of Indian descent in different parts of the empire retain the rights of the British citizen wherever they were.[53] Gandhi himself thought in terms of imperial citizenship, insisting during his years in South Africa (1893–1914) on his loyalty to the empire, enlisting Indians to serve as stretcher bearers during the Anglo-Boer War, supporting the British in putting down an African rebellion in 1906, and recruiting Indians to help save the empire in the war of 1914–18. Indians contributed extensively to the British cause in World War I, as did colonized subjects from elsewhere in the empire. Gandhi hoped that in showcasing the duties of the imperial citizen, he could press claims for the rights that status implied. But Britain refused to fulfill its wartime promises of allowing India partial self-government or to pressure the "white" dominions to allow Indians to migrate where they wished within the empire. By closing off the possibilities of imperial citizenship, the British government brought about the intensification and redirection of Indian political movements after the war (chapter 3).[54]

After the forceful incorporation of parts of West Africa into the British Empire, some activists were thinking in original ways about combining African and British modes of gover-

nance. The lawyer and journalist J. E. Casely-Hayford imagined the creation of a federation of African political communities within a British empire that accepted Africans as equals.[55]
Casely-Hayford is often seen as a pioneer of African nationalism, and he was indeed arguing for a distinctly African voice
in politics, but in the early twentieth century such arguments
could be framed within empire rather than against it. Thus
alongside the argument for a very white "Greater Britain" were
alternative concepts of imperial citizenship.

Initiatives such as Casely-Hayford's met with frustration. In
the British West Indies, meanwhile, the descendants of people
"liberated" from slavery in the 1830s continued to find themselves deprived of political rights and economic opportunities.
In the 1920s and 1930s, West Indian newspapers, petitions,
and public protests demanded that black inhabitants of British islands be treated as citizens of empire. Organizations like
the "Citizens Welfare League" or the "British Empire Citizens"
and "Workers' Home Rule Party" made their claims for rights.
These demands were deflected or denied in London. Meanwhile, attempts of citizens of color—from the West Indies as
well as from India—to enter other British territories, including Australia, Canada, and New Zealand (as well as the United
States), were met with bans, justified for example by explicitly
racist arguments. As one defender of a white Greater Britain
stated, "In my view full British citizenship, 'good' for any and
every part of the Empire and entitled to recognition by foreign
States, cannot be given to British subjects of colour."[56]

The advocates of an inclusive citizenship were running up
against an argument that linked Britishness, race, and citizenship. But it was precisely because *citizenship* was a relationship to a state and was not in itself defined by religion, race, or
ethnicity that diverse people within the empire could lay claim
to inclusion as citizens of the British Empire. If the rulers of

empire wanted their subjects to accept a place within the polity and to serve it in peace and war, they had to confront activists who made clear that their people would only do so if they had the rights of citizens.

France and Beyond: Nation, People, Empire

We turn now to a country that considers itself the cradle of citizenship—but often forgets that "nation," "people," and "citizen" were constructs that developed and were played out in the context of empire.[57] Citizenship in France before the Revolution was more a matter of distinguishing foreigners from French people than for conferring any specific rights on the latter.[58] As early as 1715, high officials of the monarchy were speaking of a body of citizens who displayed their love for their *patrie*.[59] The classic story of Enlightenment and Revolution focuses on the argument that the people's will became the basis of the nation's sovereignty. My concern is with the spatial dimensions of the story.

The boundaries of "France" were not entirely clear even before the Revolution. The French monarchy in the seventeenth and eighteenth centuries ruled not only a territory in western Europe (with all the problems it posed), but also land in North America, known as Nouvelle France, with its settler population and uneasy but vital relations with Amerindians, and the Caribbean islands, with their small planter elites of French origin and large slave population from Africa. It claimed smaller enclaves in Senegal, India, and elsewhere. In the overseas territories, the people—settlers or indigenous—were tied by vertical connection to the monarch, but they potentially could forge horizontal ties with each other or make common cause with dissident elements in metropolitan politics. Whether indigenous inhabitants of Nouvelle France should be considered

"French" if they converted to Christianity was a matter of debate on both sides of the Atlantic. Some observers in France worried that Indians would acculturate the settlers more than the other way around.[60]

The existence within Nouvelle France of coherent—even powerful—indigenous polities posed not only the danger of raids and warfare but also the possibility of cooperative relations between settler and indigenous elites and potential allies against rival empires. In the Great Lakes region of North America, Indian communities were able for a time to play off French, British, and Spanish empires' need for intermediaries, trading partners, and allies against each other. The disaster for Indian polities was that somebody won the war of 1756–63.[61] The British Empire, and even more so settlers of British origin, had a freer hand after that point.

In the plantation colonies, the subordination of the slaves was clear enough, but not so that of the *gens de couleur*, the children of French fathers and mothers of African origin. As the owners of landed property and slaves, many *gens de couleur* had a claim to be contributing to the prosperity of the empire, but they were the object of prejudice and discrimination from the white elite. Yet even the most oppressed people within the plantation order were in some sense the king's subjects. The Code Noir of 1685—a royal edict that ordered masters to feed their slaves and not punish them too barbarically (although its main concern was discipline)—implied that the king could regulate the actions of one category of French person in relation to another. French authorities had to take the code somewhat seriously for fear that a regime of pure oppression would provoke slave revolts.[62]

With the Declaration of the Rights of Man and of the Citizen in 1789, the stakes in defining the Frenchness of different peoples escalated: the citizen was now expected to have a determining voice in the affairs of state. Here we run into a problem in writing the history of citizenship. An idealized reading of the French pattern is frequently taken for the essence of what citizenship is, conflating nation, popular sovereignty, and citizenship. In some readings, the citizen is necessarily an autonomous individual, freed of constraints of estate, clan, or caste and interacting with the state.[63]

If one doesn't take the conflation for granted, one can probe the relationship among these dimensions. The sociologist Michael Mann distinguishes among different "ruling class strategies" of citizenship. The liberal variant emphasizes the individual as political and economic actor (as in British liberalism); a more social conception (the model of Bismarckian Germany) entails a top-down strategy to provide a modicum of security to workers and peasants while limiting their political input; an authoritarian model (found in nineteenth-century monarchies and twentieth-century dictatorships) emphasizes the belonging of a body of citizens to a state, with limited rights; and a final pattern, including France, produces persistent and unresolved debate and conflict between elite and popular power, with struggles over election rules, trade union rights, and social policy.[64]

Interlude: Capitalism and Citizenship

Overlapping the French and English focus on the individual political actor is the question of the individual economic actor. The relationship of these two questions is a concern in political theory, and it was a concern of political thinkers going back to the eighteenth century. To say that a person's property is to be protected is to assume a relationship of an individual object and an individual person, recognized by a body capable of both power and authority, in other words a state.[65] In the arguments of Locke and others, citizens—active citizens at least—should be property owners. The right to property figured prominently in the key texts of the French and American revolutions.

The significance of property to the development of capitalism is not just about those who possess it, but those who do not, the large class of people who have no access to the means of production and who must therefore sell their labor power. Capitalist development, in Marx's analysis, depended on the creation of a class of people who, whatever access to land they or their ancestors once had, no longer had such rights; they were expropriable, expellable, and not just through brute force but with the legitimacy of the law. In assuring propertyless citizens of the equal protection of the law for something they did not have, a citizenship regime provided a legitimate basis for a system of formal equality and actual inequality, while also setting out a terrain on which the relationship of the two could be debated.

Capitalist development also positioned the wage worker in relation to the state, via laws against vagrancy, poor laws, supervision of labor organization, wage and hour rules, and the regulation or repression of collective action. The very notion that labor exists as anonymous labor power, for sale in the market rather than nested in complex social relations, also sets out an individual in relation to the state. The worker was an object of surveillance and possible punishment, but he or she was also protected against enslavement. With the development of industry, states became increasingly concerned that unmediated exploitation could produce a dangerous class. European elites took different approaches—some more repressive, some more inclusionary—to define and channel workers' potential actions.[66]

The citizenship concept tended to dissolve the worker—like any other social category—into the citizenry as a whole. This posed a challenge to labor movement leaders: should they mobilize workers around specific interests or in the name of the general interest? It poses a dilemma that is with us today: whether to look at the body politic as an aggregation of individuals or as a socially complex entity in which different parts are positioned differently.[67] Capitalist development thus gives rise to particular tensions in the politics of citizenship.

Back to France: Nation, Empire, Citizenship, 1789–1914

We return to the distinctions made within the apparently leveling category of citizenship. Pierre Rosanvallon insists that "equality was the 'mother-idea'" of the revolutionary process—equality in the sense of the equivalence of all citizens, the autonomy (freedom from dependence) of each citizen, and equal participation of citizens in politics. Yet in Paris during the Revolution, the constituent assemblies distinguished between an "active," male, citizen and a "passive" citizen, whose person and property were protected by the rights regime but who did not participate in politics.[68] The supposed dependence of wives on husbands rationalized their exclusion. Servants and apprentices were excluded from active citizenship as well, because of their dependence on their masters. Rosanvallon writes that the idea of universal suffrage "was not even thinkable in 1789."[69]

It became so through the political conflicts and claim-making of the nineteenth century. Claim-making was a two-way street, for during much of the nineteenth century French elites—landed and industrial—strove to counter the influence of workers and peasants. Gender remained a controversial category even when universal male suffrage became the law. Only in 1944 did the female half of the population acquire the vote.

It took 155 years for the ideal of universal citizenship to become universal suffrage in France—in European France, that is.

This limitation brings us back to the relationship of citizenship, nation, and empire.[70] To some, the French "nation" was a bounded entity located in Europe.[71] But the boundedness of the revolutionary "nation" was thrown open by events in the empire. In 1789, the white plantation owners of Saint Domingue—France's richest colony, the world's greatest producer of sugar, and the home to thousands of slaves, mostly African-born, living and working under miserable conditions—sent representatives to Paris to insist that the rights of the citizen applied to them. Moreover, they demanded the right to govern their own colony, since the conditions of a slave society were not familiar to metropolitan legislators. After that intervention in the revolutionary debates came a delegation from the *gens de couleur*—mixed-race people—claiming that they too should have the full rights of citizens. The assemblies in Paris could not make up their mind about these demands. Then, in 1791, a slave revolt erupted in Saint Domingue. Among the complex strands of this revolt was a demand by slaves for freedom and citizenship.

The revolutionary government in Saint Domingue in the early 1790s was threatened by royalist reaction, the invasion of rival empires, and the slave revolt. In this situation, the Republic decided—for pragmatic reasons and not just revolutionary rigor—to grant citizenship rights to free *gens de couleur* in 1792 and finally, in 1793, to free the slaves and make them citizens. The Republic hoped to create an army of citizens to defend the Revolution. The Revolution, like most social movements that advance very far, brought together people across social categories without ending the conflicts and tensions among them.[72]

Empire citizenship was terminated by Napoleon, who reinstated slavery in 1802. At that point revolutionaries in Saint

Domingue turned from remaking France toward exiting from it. Napoleon's army was defeated by a combination of rebel armies and tropical microbes. The proclamation of the independent republic of Haiti in 1804 was the counter to Napoleon's restoration of slavery in other French colonies in the Caribbean. Post-Napoleonic, like pre-revolutionary, France would govern its colonies by "special laws," although exceptions and controversies would repeatedly complicate the distinction between the French person in colonies and metropole. Haiti, for its part, repudiated in a firm manner the world of enslavement and colonial oppression from which it had emerged. Article 3 of its constitution of 1805 proclaimed that "The citizens of Hayti are brothers at home; equality in the eyes of the law is incontestably acknowledged."

France itself was governed by men calling themselves king or emperor for three quarters of the post-revolutionary century. Except for the periods of republican government, a monarch ruled in the name of the people rather than the people ruling, allowing only limited forms of legislative input. Even after republican rule was established in 1871, there remained an enduring tension between "the people as a nation, as an abstraction," and the people as they actually were, divided by origins, gender, religion, and class.[73] While the left of the political spectrum has long feared that such divisions would obstruct popular unity, the right has feared unity and sought means to temper its potential. With the changing composition of the French population, the tension between universality and singularity on the one hand and particularity on the other has produced considerable brittleness in France's political life.

Post-revolutionary France produced two innovations that would have a durable—but not consistent—impact on the question of citizenship: the *état civil* (1792) and the civil code (1803). The *état civil* was a system of population registration, intended to apply to all citizens, that took the place of baptismal and other religious records. In it were compulsorily recorded, so that the state would know, evidence of each individual's birth, marriage, and death. By the inscription of such acts before a state official, the individual "became a member of the civil community." The *état civil* gave substance and symbolism to the individual's direct relation to the state, independent of any status group (estate) or religious affiliation.[74] A person could produce extracts from the *état civil* if he or she needed to prove citizenship, age, marital status, or inheritance rights. It thus became the basis by which people could claim the right to vote and later the right to education or social benefits. The *état civil* was not simply an instrument of state surveillance but a means by which citizens claimed entitlements.[75]

For this reason, there is something poignant about the discovery of Laurent Dubois, looking at records from Guadeloupe during the brief period when the slaves were freed and before they were re-enslaved, that ex-slaves were eager to have themselves inscribed in the *état civil*.[76] They wanted their names to be written down, as individuals, as people who belonged to society, whose birth, marital status, and death mattered, in relation to a place and to a state, whereas in the past they had only been recorded as someone's property.[77]

The other instrument for marking the place of the citizen in society, the civil code, helped not only to define who was French but to spell out how people could be French. It regulated marriage, filiation, inheritance, and other civil matters; not just monogamy but the superior position of the male as household head were enshrined in the civil code.[78] French rules under the code for deciding who was a citizen stressed *jus sanguinis*, the family link through the father, to previous generations of French people.[79] A law of 1851, firmed up under the Third Republic in 1889, introduced the principle of double *jus soli*: someone born on French soil of parents at least one of whom was also born in France was automatically French; anyone else would have to go through a procedure to establish French nationality, in some cases a declaration, in others a fully vetted process of naturalization. Behind this law—frequently revised—was a desire for France to have more citizens—but not necessarily from its colonies.[80]

In 1848, during another revolutionary outbreak in European France, the state abolished slavery, this time for good. Ex-slaves became citizens rather than being slotted into an intermediate category, but not quite equal ones. Even French politicians who denied thinking of ex-slaves as racially inferior worried that the experience of enslavement had made them incapable of acting in the rational manner expected of citizens. Just who could vote and for what was contested, and while representatives of the plantation islands did sit in the legislature in Paris, the islands themselves were governed under a special regime. The elected deputies, as Silyane Larcher puts it, were voting for laws "that, without special and exceptional dispositions, were not applied to the colony that elected them."[81]

In 1830, as France began its conquest of Algeria, officials initially claiming to respect the arrangements of the previous imperial ruler—the Ottoman Empire—insisted that Muslims could keep their status under Islamic law. But as the conquest of the region proceeded with escalating violence and as the government promoted the settlement of people of Christian confession from around the Mediterranean to create the nucleus of a settler society under French control, recognition of difference turned into a regime of invidious distinction.

The colonization of Algeria was initiated by the monarchies that ruled France from the fall of Napoleon until 1848.[82] The republic that briefly followed the revolution of that year, while making citizens out of the slaves of the Caribbean, declared

Algeria to be an integral part of the Republic without making clear what this meant for its diverse peoples. It was the Second Empire (1852–70) that brought clarity to the situation—in the terms of a frankly self-proclaimed empire. Napoleon III famously said, "Algeria is not a colony, properly speaking, but an Arab kingdom.... The natives have an equal right to my protection and I am as much the emperor of the Arabs as the emperor of the French."[83]

Meanwhile, in metropolitan France the Second Empire witnessed the "thickening" of the concept of citizenship: a "general stirring of civic activism" among opponents of the government, richer associational life, a wider range of publicly expressed ideological viewpoints, debates over the decentralization of power, increased literacy, and broadened suffrage and frequent elections. Tensions between popular influence and top-down efforts to contain social change remained at the crux of politics.[84] The Second Empire, with its explicit acceptance that different people were governed differently, could both entertain a complex debate over what citizenship meant in the metropole and insist that millions of people were French but excluded from citizenship.

Ever since the Revolution, the relationship of nationality and citizenship has moved in different directions. When the French government in the 1790s made all people who were in one way or another French into citizens, nationality and citizenship converged. When Napoleon I reinstated slavery, the two categories diverged. Napoleon III kept the two apart, but gave all nationals the possibility, in theory, of becoming citizens. In the republic that succeeded the Second Empire the distinction was maintained, but it became a source of controversy between those who thought a republic could not divide French people this way and those who saw governing different people differently as the normal and necessary practice of empires. The relationship of nationality and citizenship would be reconfigured again after 1945.

At home, French lawmakers in the late nineteenth century proved adept at making distinctions between a responsible, socially integrated citizen and that citizen's "others"—the criminal, the foreigner, the dangerous classes. In regard to the empire, the legal texts avoided explicit mention of "race," but made personal status the basis of exclusion from the category of citizen.[85] In Algeria, the argument that Muslims could not be citizens because their status came under Islamic law was initially mirrored by the exclusion of Jews on the basis of their adhesion to Mosaic law. But in 1870 a new decree placed Jews collectively under the civil code and in the category of citizen. Muslim Algerians, on the contrary, would have to apply as individuals—renouncing their "Islamic" personal status—if they wished to become citizens. Few wanted to do so; fewer still were accepted as citizens. The "colons"—settlers of European origin—of Algeria made full use of their own status as citizens to keep Muslim subjects a clearly demarcated—and denigrated—population.[86]

The Third Republic differed from the Second Empire in that at least some of its leading actors agonized over deviations from republican universality even if they ended up maintaining the imperial principle and practice of governing different people differently.[87] That colonial subjects could become citizens collectively was not excluded, but it was deferred indefinitely, pending their assimilation to French ways. In the 1880s and during World War I some important politicians argued (unsuccessfully) for giving Muslim Algerians citizenship rights without their coming under the civil code. But the question of equal political rights kept coming back, in the demands of Algerians and among some French legislators themselves.[88]

Exclusion from citizenship meant more than the lack of full political representation and the absence of freedom of association and of speech. French subjects, in Algeria and colonies acquired later in the nineteenth century, came under the *indigénat*, decrees that enabled the local administrator—acting as prosecutor and judge—to condemn subjects for a wide range of offenses. It left Muslim Algerians with few means to resist land-grabbing by European settlers or demands for forced labor. French subjects lived alongside others who had rights they could not have.[89]

The decades just before and after 1900 were a time when the Frenchness of people in European France was being imposed at the expense of regional cultural distinctions and loyalties. In Eugen Weber's famous account, school and army were crucial mechanisms for the integration of citizens. Civic education—making people into capable citizens—became a prime duty of the state. In Algeria, some Muslims went into military service and many went to school, but in this context these institutions reflected and reinforced rather than reduced distinctions.[90]

Yet another variation on the citizenship regime applied in the Quatre Communes of Senegal, four small port towns that had been enclave colonies since the seventeenth century. Given the small French presence, officials needed to secure the attachment of the local inhabitants of these entrepôts—known as *originaires*—and conveyed some of the rights of the citizen to them, but without requiring that they come under the French civil code. Their affairs of marriage and inheritance were regulated by Islamic law and Islamic courts. After the reforms of 1848, men from these enclaves could vote in elections to local councils and the National Assembly in Paris. As Mamadou Diouf argues, the inhabitants of the Quatre Communes used their rights to defend their distinct way of life, not to submerge themselves in the anonymity of Frenchness. It remained controversial whether they were to be considered "citoyens" or "électeurs"—voters—but they did have rights on terms different from other French people, a possible model for other parts of the empire.[91]

The trend, however, was in the opposite direction. With the violent conquest of the interior of Africa, the French government was intent on defining the distinct and inferior place of the "indigène" in most of the continent. Africans were imagined to be confined by "custom" to a way of life unassimilable to French notions, perhaps one day to be educated and elevated but for the foreseeable future to be obedient subjects whose contribution to the empire would be labor and exportable commodities.[92] In metropolitan France itself, the "abstract egalitarianism" of republican doctrine was opposed by ideologues who sought to invigorate a "French race" by encouraging natality and opposing immigration—European as well as nonwhite—consigning women to the role of mothers.[93]

The egalitarian and particularistic currents were in conflict with each other and subject to the vagaries of history. During World War I, a more inclusionary conception of citizenship carried weight. The representative of the *originaires* of Senegal to the National Assembly, Blaise Diagne, devoted much effort to recruiting African soldiers for the war effort, insisting—successfully—that *originaires* serve in regular regiments alongside other citizens and that the legislature affirm once and for all that the *originaires* were indeed citizens independent of their personal status. After the war, soldiers from other parts of Africa claimed the rights of citizens on the basis of having paid the "blood tax." The administration backpedaled, asserting that citizenship would only alienate Africans from their own culture.[94]

The notorious distinction between subject and citizen, often cited as the basic characteristic of the colonial situation, was thus as insidious as it is usually portrayed, but not so fixed an attribute. It was manipulable from above as governments adjusted their policies to the demands and threats intrinsic to holding together a diverse and unequal polity, and it was the object of claim-making from below.

European Variations

France at the turn of the twentieth century was an empire among empires. Great Britain, Germany, Austro-Hungary, Russia, Italy, Belgium, Spain, and Portugal all confronted questions of how to define—perhaps to integrate, perhaps to exclude—different peoples in their empires. This was also an era of migration, including considerable movement within Europe. The question of who could *become* a citizen was posed every day, within the continent as well as in relation to overseas populations. A rich literature—containing more than a few controversies—focuses on the variations on citizenship within Europe.[95]

Let us take the example of Germany. The contrast often made between a Germany that saw citizenship in terms of *jus sanguinis* and France, which did so in terms of *jus soli,* has turned out to be too simple; both citizenship regimes had elements of each and altered policies for fear that the other might acquire more citizens.[96] Germany, after 1871, was itself an amalgam of states, and the *Länder* (provinces) retained the right to process citizenship applications, subject to each other's review. Rivalry with the French—and memories of the conquests of the first Napoleon—fostered among part of the German elite a desire to claim "uniqueness" against the political and universalistic self-definition of mid-nineteenth-century

France.[97] There was a general reluctance in Bismarckian Germany to naturalize foreigners, but here too there were variations; Prussia was at times more willing to do so than Bavaria.

The Kaiserreich, configured in 1871, contained not only German speakers, but Polish, Danish, and French speakers. Poles were the object of particular anxiety in high places, for they were both necessary for Germany's labor force in agriculture and industry and seen by many as alien if not inferior. Even if the state resisted naturalizing Polish "foreigners," many Poles—some 2.5 million—came with the territory that the Reich claimed. Poles faced the denial of equality and exclusion from social institutions, but also efforts at assimilating them to German culture. Jewish immigration was suppressed by the authorities, but Germany's substantial Jewish population was both relatively assimilated to German culture and relatively well positioned in some sectors of the economy—a situation that encouraged rather than reduced anti-Semitism. At the same time, the creation of an explicitly German empire did not entail the absorption of all German speakers—a fourth of ethnic Germans lived outside the state that was created in 1871.[98] Even after defeating the Austrian Empire in the war of 1866, the Prussian leadership had not sought to incorporate that empire's German-speaking population into the regime. The Reich did provide a direct route via *jus sanguinis* to the recognition of citizenship for Germans who had lived outside its borders and wished to move into Germany. The government was well aware of the advantages, in its demographic contest with France, of integrating immigrants it regarded as German from the Russian or Austro-Hungarian empires and of maintaining ties with the many Germans who had left for North or South America or to colonies (not just Germany's).

Citizenship legislation in Germany reflected not so much a consensus on maintaining a coherent sense of "Germanness" as strong disagreement over prioritizing ethnocultural solidarity and the need for workers and soldiers.[99] Citizenship, before World War I, existed within a regime that muted the political voice of the average citizen. After 1919, citizenship questions were caught up in conflict and mobilization from the extreme left, the extreme right, and everything in between. Widespread deprivation and loss of imperial prestige as well as extensive immigration from the east challenged many citizens' sense of what it meant to be German.[100] The entrepreneurs of racialized politics in the 1920s had something to draw on in promoting an ethnonationalist version of what it meant to be German, but those tendencies had up to that point existed in relation to a politics of pragmatic acceptance of imperial inclusivity and a cosmopolitan elite culture. It was in the context of the late 1920s and early 1930s that the Nazis' exclusionary definition of the *Volk* took root, followed by the stripping away of all citizens' rights to political participation. Out of this cauldron emerged the racist Nuremberg laws of 1935 and the genocide.

What did the overseas colonies that Germany acquired, trying to catch up with Britain and France from the 1880s, signify for the forceful incorporation of different people into an imperial system? The war of extermination that it conducted against the resistance to conquest of the Herero people of Southwest Africa has received well-deserved opprobrium. After the equally brutal repression of a revolt in Tanganyika in 1905, the government recognized that it had to live off its colonized population, not destroy it. It pulled back from policies of forced cultivation and forced labor for German plantations and began to encourage peasant production, and it had to find means to define Africans' place in a society that was highly unequal but offered a degree of judicial protection.[101]

The earliest German explorers, traders, and settlers frequently had sexual relations, occasionally even marriages, with indigenous women. The resulting children gave rise to the question of whether the masculine prerogative of acknowledging offspring—and therefore defining them as "German"—should receive state recognition or whether the purity of the German *Volk* should be defended against such dilution. The latter position was advocated by German women's organizations in the colonies and at home, but it also resonated with an increasing bourgeois vision of colonial society that was not unique to Germany—a notion of properly restrained sexual conduct and a society of sharply defined racial borders. Anti-miscegenation regulation was a way of marking a boundary, but the amount of attention given to a small group of people who fell between racial categories was a sign of anxiety over the frontiers of citizenship.[102]

How German administrators actually ruled varied greatly within Africa and even more between colonies in Africa, Asia, and the Pacific. Officials, as in French and British colonies, had to come to grips with the limits of their power and their need to work through vertical hierarchies of African societies if they were to bring power down to village level.[103] The racialized thinking and forms of exclusion directed against Poles and Jews during the Kaiserreich overlapped with racialization in the colonies, but, as recent scholarship has suggested, one has to be careful about drawing too direct a line between the particularities of German citizenship regimes in the period before 1914 and those after 1933.[104] Who is excluded from a community of citizens and who can struggle for inclusion is shaped in a dynamic way; these are not fixed or inherent characteristics of "Germany" or any other political entity.

In most of Europe, citizenship in a nation and citizenship in an empire were in ambiguous and often tense relationship to each other. Nationalist movements could pull an empire apart or—as in Austria-Hungary in 1867—give rise to creative efforts to conjugate recognized national communities with an imperial state and a common citizenship, or it could be a force for aggression and the subordination of others.[105] The late nineteenth century was a time of extensive migration within Europe and beyond, hence of people claiming citizenship in new places. Governments' desire for more workers to staff growing industries and men to serve as soldiers stood in tension with fears of newcomers and pressures to privilege long-time citizens' access to newly created social benefits. Movement and mixing posed problems both to trade unions trying to organize people on the basis of the solidarities of class or occupation and to governing elites trying to promote linguistic homogenization and civic pride. The end of the nineteenth century, which appears at first glance to be an age of national consolidation, was at the same time "the age of diversification of belonging." It was also a time when some European elites were trying—in vain it turned out in 1914—to encourage internationalism, through the development of international organizations and international law.[106]

In the jockeying for power in late-nineteenth-century Europe, the empires of Russia, Austro-Hungary, and the Ottomans were still major players, if not what they had once been. France, Great Britain, Germany, and others with overseas colonies had to make effective use of their combinations of citizens and subjects and contain dangers arising at home and abroad. Advocates of a purely national conception of society could argue that a homogeneous citizenry would be stronger than empires with a diverse mixture of citizens and subjects, but that was not the way inter-state politics was being conducted.[107] At the same time, movements within European states were making claims *as citizens*—for more political voice, for a decent standard of living, for social benefits—and in the empires, movements among subjects were making demands to *become* citizens.

Modes of Belonging

What do the politics of incorporation and citizenship look like beyond western Europe? And how, as European power extended further, were these citizenship regimes challenged and perhaps transformed?

The Ottoman Empire in the nineteenth century is a good site for thinking about these questions. Engin Isin warns against either measuring Ottoman citizenship against an allegedly western Europe standard of citizenship or pretending that Ottoman practices actually approached those of western Europe. But how was the act of political belonging constituted in an Ottoman context? Not as an unchanging, inherently "Ottoman" way.[108]

The 600-year-long history of the Ottoman Empire does not suggest that this empire was incapable of capturing the political imagination of its subjects. The Ottoman polity relied on a balance between recognition of the integrity and relative autonomy of its multiple parts, defined most often in religious terms, and a powerful household directly controlled by the sultan. The people who actually ran the empire did not come from the sultan's kinsmen; they were not necessarily of "Turkish" origin. The anti-aristocratic bias of the Ottoman polity distinguished itself from the great empires of fifteenth–eighteenth-century Europe, including that of the Habsburgs.

For the most part, the leaders of religious groups managed the internal affairs of their communities as long as they were obedient and paid their taxes.[109] Ottoman cities from the fifteenth to the early nineteenth century, particularly the ports, were populated by Muslims of various origins and different legal traditions; by Jews, Greeks, and Armenians; by Balkan communities; by people from an even wider array of linguistic and cultural distinct groups throughout the empire; and by travelers from many regions with whom the Ottomans actively traded. The leaders of these communities participated in councils and consultations with the sultanate. They had the right to petition the sultan. In other words, "belonging" within the Ottoman Empire did not entail mere physical presence or even tolerance. People were bound to the state not as equivalent individuals but as members of a mosaic of collectivities, each with its political hierarchy. What leaders and members of a religious or other community might expect was not equality with each other or with Muslims and certainly not an equal voice in governance, but rather protection and access, in some form, to judicial institutions.

Hierarchy was enforced by a structure of power that stood alongside communal incorporation. The sultan developed a powerful instrument of recruitment and control that put people in positions of authority precisely because their social connections were weak. Under the *devshirme* system, young boys, particularly from Christian families in the Balkans, were forcefully recruited at a young age, converted to Islam, and trained for either military roles (the Janissaries) or administrative service. Even the vizier, the second most powerful man of the empire, was recruited this way. The sultan himself was born of outside connections. Once the regime had consolidated itself, the sultan did not marry but produced his heirs through concubines—girls taken as captives, often from the Caucasus or Ukraine. By reproducing itself through concubinage the sultanate avoided the danger of empowered in-laws.[110]

After the Ottoman conquest of the holy lands of Islam early in the sixteenth century, the sultan gave himself the title of

Caliph, the leader of the Islamic world. This added a religious and ideological foundation to belonging to an empire that by then had acquired a geographic scale approaching that of the Roman Empire. Until at least the middle of the nineteenth century, the multiconfessional and Islamic characters of the empire were complementary. In addition to the vertical channels of power that linked the sultan to religious communities and a dependent household were other sorts of power relations in towns of the Ottoman Empire, conducted through guilds, councils, and a tradition of consulting with the "notables" of each community. Guilds, for example, could to a degree control affairs within their professional domain and petition the government in regard to taxation or other issues; they occasionally staged rebellions; they also provided for their members in need.[111] There is no need to pretend that the Ottoman Empire had produced "civil society"—the concept is problematic enough for western Europe—but a contrast between a starkly authoritarian east and a civil order emerging out of urban ties in the west is much too simple.[112]

The Ottoman Empire was never self-contained, but constituted a crucial link between the western and eastern parts of Eurasia, with close trade and travel connections in both directions. That meant that new ideas would not be long in coming. New ideas and new connections would be a challenge to a political system that stressed the linkage of groups to the sultan.

Jews, Greeks, and Armenians had long profited from their recognition within the empire and from their networks extending beyond it. But by the nineteenth century, more of them were finding that networks could be forged that did not pass through Istanbul. The challenge posed by western European empires was not only their rising economic—and hence military—capacity, but also their ability to penetrate the relationships on which belonging had been developed within the Ottoman Empire. Communities within Ottoman cities could develop links to French, British, Italian, or other consuls, who could provide legal protection and sometimes arms to people who claimed to share a religion or even a nationality with the intruding power. France, Britain, and other foreign powers found that extending protection—to Jews as well as fellow Christians— gave the protecting country a set of connections in Ottoman lands and the protected person the possibility of multiple networks and multiple means of support in case of conflict. People were situating themselves in relation to different states, and their loyalties became of increasing concern to Ottoman rulers in the nineteenth century.[113] The Ottoman Empire responded with new initiatives.

In the 1830s, the Ottoman Empire embarked upon reforms, known as the *Tanzimat*, that posited the direct adherence of all subjects of the sultan to the Ottoman polity, not passing through a religious community. This conception was elaborated in a nationality law of 1869 that imposed a form of *jus soli*, with elements of *jus sanguinis* in the paternal line. The law articulated a clear distinction between an Ottoman population and foreigners. It was intended to rectify a situation in which people tried at various times to claim the protection of both the sultan and a foreign consulate. Whether these rules should be considered "citizenship" is controversial, but they did imply the existence a horizontal category of "Ottomans" not mediated by the vertical relationship of communities through their leaders to the sultan.[114] The reformers wanted the individual Ottoman to see him or herself in relation to the state; they were trying to foster Ottoman patriotism, not to give citizens a fully array of political rights.[115] But the reforms also enabled people, as Ottomans, to make legal claims and to set out demands and arguments in newspapers and other media.

A Parliament with appointed representatives sat from 1876 to 1878, when the sultan shut it down. It was reopened, this time with elected representatives, in 1908. The history of representative government in the empire was a checkered one, but the reforms had an important impact even when the sultan refused to recognize parliamentary authority. The mere fact of being represented by deputies—and the fact that a significant minority of the deputies were Christians and Jews—made a point. The reforms of the nineteenth century also included ending tax farming (although it crept back) and instituted universal military service. Education was encouraged—including western-style courses—and graduates had a chance to compete for posts in the bureaucracy. The sultanate developed ceremonies to emphasize the direct relation of individuals to the realm as a whole.[116]

The Tanzimat reforms created tensions, for they compromised the old ways of governing, giving citizens new ways to pose demands without necessarily providing the government with the means to satisfy them.[117] Reform produced losers who had once embodied the hierarchy of sultanic service, notably the Janissaries, the military corps recruited from outside the empire's heartland and given a military education and who were supplanted by a professional army based on conscription from all around the empire. Janissaries revolted in 1807, forced the sultan to reach a compromise with them, but were eliminated in a bloody fashion in 1826. Ali Yaycioglu sees a transition in the early nineteenth century from "a vertical empire" to "a horizontal and participatory empire," followed after considerable pushback by a structure that mixed generalized citizenship with vertical relations between the sultan and regional elites.[118] All this was occurring in the context of heightened challenges on several fronts: rebellion in Greece and the Balkans assisted by Britain, Russia, and other rival empires, loss of North African territories to France and Italy, financial crises, a drive for autonomy by the Ottoman governor of Egypt, disaffection by educated elites imbued with "liberal" ideas, tension between an autocratic Sultan and constitutionally minded elites.[119]

In response to the incursions of European empires into the Middle East, the Ottoman Empire tightened its grip on relatively distant regions like Yemen and asserted its own version of a civilizing mission. Even in areas in recently subdued parts of Yemen where people were considered backward, the Ottoman regime did not try to make a rigid distinction between rights-bearing citizens and uncivilized subjects, instead providing for the representation of Yemen in the Ottoman Parliament in 1876–78 and after 1908. While trying to underscore that the people of Yemen, like those of Syria, Egypt, or Anatolia, were citizens of empire and had a stake in its institutions, officials were careful to work with local elites, avoiding some of the standardizing practices of government imposed elsewhere (censuses, conscription, uniform judicial institutions), in short trying to find "the 'right' measure of difference" in the practice of governance.[120]

Ottomanism had considerable staying power, an amalgam of old loyalties and new strategies to secure loyalty through the citizenship construct. Michelle Campos's research on Palestine reveals strong evidence from the beginning of the twentieth century of people's self-identification as both Palestinian and Ottoman citizens. It was on this dual basis that Palestinian elites claimed rights within the empire. Meanwhile, Jews in the empire debated in their own newspapers what it meant to be Jewish and Ottoman and demanded fuller representation in Ottoman councils and civil service positions. In the difficult case of Egypt, where the Ottoman governor Mehmet Ali established de facto autonomy from the 1830s, Will Hanley describes persistent notions of "overlapping sovereignties" and a "performative" concept of citizenship.[121] Even after Greece became independent of Ottoman rule in 1830, many Greeks continued to migrate to Anatolia and remained an important part of the Ottoman economy and society until the early twentieth century.[122] One might see in Ottoman history between 1830 and World War I an example of "multilevel citizenship" or "multicultural citizenship" advocated by some scholars today (Introduction)—an example of its possibilities and a warning of its limitations and dangers.

Ottoman reforms did not overcome rivalries and tensions within and among communities. After the empire lost most of its largely Christian provinces and after waves of expulsions in both directions following wars in the Balkans in 1876–78 and again in 1912–13, it became an increasingly Islamic polity, and parts of its Turkish-speaking elite began to develop an increasingly Turkish sense of entitlement, challenging the pragmatic inclusivity that had characterized the empire. The Ottoman Empire took in a vast number of Muslim refugees from the Crimean War of 1854–56, the Ottoman-Russo War and Balkan Wars of 1877–79, and Russian conquests in Caucasus later in the century, producing a resettlement crisis that fostered tensions with remaining Christian communities even as the empire was losing territory.[123]

It was especially after the Balkan Wars of 1912–13 that the mutual toleration of Greeks and Muslim Ottomans in Anatolia broke down, presaging the massive population exchange that would take place after World War I.[124] During the war, the nationalizing, Turkifying trend within a powerful faction of the Ottoman leadership was responsible for the genocidal massacre of Armenians, the most desperate and ugly action of a polity that was no longer fully Ottoman and not yet Turkish.[125] At the same time, much of the elite in the Arab provinces displayed until the very end of the war a willingness to link their fortunes—and their claim-making—to the empire. The Committee of Union and Progress that came to rule the empire after 1908 had to compromise its homogenizing ideology with deals with local elites.[126]

Citizenship in the Ottoman Empire had been a changing construct, and different segments of the empire's elites, at the end of its long historical trajectory, showed themselves capable of seeing beyond an ethnic definition of belonging or else carrying exclusion to a murderous degree.[127] The breakdown of the Ottoman attempt of the mid-nineteenth century to develop a common Ottoman citizenship out of a religiously diverse population was not simply the result of nationalist mobilizations, but of other empires (British, Russian, Habsburg) that used different national communities as proxies in their interempire conflicts. The Balkan Wars and the ethnic cleansing they fostered, the massacres of Armenians in the 1890s and the genocide of 1915, and the mutual expulsions of Greek-Turkish populations after World War I were as much the cause as the consequence of the crystallization of ethnonational blocks in the eastern Mediterranean and Balkans. Since the fourteenth century, the Ottoman Empire had developed its own ways of balancing difference and belonging, and it had adapted over centuries to changing pressures from within and without, providing the context in which different communities themselves evolved. Whether the ethnic attachments of different peoples who had once peopled the Ottoman Empire would eventually have doomed its experiment in common but differentiated citizenship we cannot tell. Neither the Ottoman Empire nor the fledgling notions of citizenship that shaped the give-and-take of politics from the Tanzimat to World War I died a natural death. They were the casualties of inter-empire conflict and of world war, as different imperial powers made use of their citizens and subjects in their quests for power and their rivalries with each other.

Citizenship in a New Century

In 1900, the Ottoman, Russian, German, and Austro-Hungarian empires, as well as the French and British, were major actors on the world scene, and neither the model of a nation-state, with its defined borders and putatively homogeneous citizenry, nor the model of a colonial empire, with its sharp distinction between citizens who participate in a political process and subjects who are excluded, can account for the actual dynamics of political processes of that time. The imperial polities proved capable of mobilizing a significant proportion of their citizens to fight in a highly destructive war in 1914–18. Whatever the problems of the "old" empires, it was not clear in 1914 that their political model was exhausted. These empires were, in different ways, the losers of a war in which the winners were also—and more effectively—mobilizing the human and material resources of empire.

By the early twentieth century, the state in Europe was coming to mean more than belonging, loyalty, taxes, and military service. Citizenship was taking on a new significance in the European portions of some of the empires, and that was to have an important impact throughout the empires a half century and a second world war later: citizenship was becoming a basis for social welfare programs. Some welfare systems evolved in the context of an evolving, increasingly popular electorate, slowly providing the basis for social democracy; others, as in Bismarck's Germany, were top-down initiatives intended to stave off challenges to an authoritarian state. Welfare states

reflect less demands grabbed from below by mobilizing popular elements than compromises among class- or occupation-
based organizations and political parties uncertain of their
social basis.[128]

The conventional argument is that the advent of social benefits in the states of western Europe resulted in the tightening
of legal and administrative mechanisms for deciding who was
a citizen and restricting the access of noncitizens to those benefits, if not to the territory. The increasing use of passports and
the imposition of immigration controls were part of the process.[129] There is much to these arguments, but the actual story
is more complicated. European governments worried that too
sharp a distinction between social benefits accorded workers
who were citizens and noncitizen workers from other European countries could cause social and diplomatic difficulties.
Where immigration was restricted, the application of the law
could vary. In the case of France, not only could workers from
Italy or elsewhere find ways to get around restrictions, but
elements of the business community in some cities or regions
and even state officials could be happy to see them do so.[130]

As in the wealthier states of Europe, immigration into the
United States was both economically vital and politically contentious. But the exclusionary dimension of citizenship was
strongest when it came to non-European immigration. The
anti-Asian measures taken in the United States from the late
nineteenth century onward reflected the possibility that significant numbers of Asians were insinuating themselves into
American society and might even acquire, like other immigrants, a basis as rights-bearing individuals. Doubts about the
American colonization of the Philippines arose because of fears
that Filipinos might become de facto citizens of the United
States, or at least people who, even if subordinated, could be
Americans and nothing else, as eventually proved to be the

case with Puerto Ricans.[131] Important parts of the Chinese diaspora, meanwhile, were engaged both in setting down roots in different parts of the world—and finding ways around restrictive immigration rules—and in maintaining ties to China, including providing some of the funding and support for the nationalist movement of Sun Yat-Sen. The anthropologist Aiwa Ong has deployed the concept of "flexible citizenship" to characterize the multiple affinities that Chinese, in the present, try to maintain while in motion around the world. Citizenship, as she makes clear, is not infinitely flexible, and people in motion—Chinese or otherwise—encounter barriers to entry into some countries and risk being treated as less than a full member of society in others.[132]

Citizenship a century ago was not necessarily rigid and not necessarily national. Within Europe and beyond, the space of political belonging had been repeatedly transformed over the centuries, but not in a single direction. The interplay of city, lordship, and monarchy of fourteenth-century Iberia had given rise in new parts of the empire to the subordination of conquered people within a structure of power articulated through vassalage, Catholic monarchy, and a social order that placed Spaniards and Indians in unequal communities and placed slaves on the outside of such an order. The impact of ideas and practices of popular sovereignty and constitutional governance in the late eighteenth and early nineteenth centuries opened the way to momentous political conflict and change, and the possibility of a government chosen by its citizens forced confrontation with the location of that citizenship in imperial, colonial, and national space—a conflict played out with high drama in Spanish, British, and French empires. The Ottoman and other empires, with their distinct notions of political belonging, would soon face the question of whether political belonging was mediated by communities of different sorts or implied direct embrace of a singular political unit, with rights and duties focused on a state.

Those encounters and revolutions did not resolve the problem of who could participate in a community of citizens, even as information about democracy and citizenship was communicated around much of the world through lines that imperial power had laid down or via networks developed by opponents of the imperial status quo. The new discourses meant that the problem had to be confronted. In different places within colonial empires, slaves, freed people of African descent, and indigenous communities refused to accept that the rights of the citizen did not apply to them. In the Ottoman and Austro-Hungarian empires, liberal ideas of a universal citizenship clashed with long-standing arrangements that had assured different confessional communities a place in a political entity that gave their elites, at least, possibilities for commercial, social, and political connections across a wide space. These empires sometimes found creative solutions to such tensions of empire—the Ottoman nationality law of 1869 or the dual monarchy of Austria-Hungary in 1867—but the tensions did not disappear. Even the sharp, racialized distinctions made in the colonial empires of France, Britain, Germany, and Portugal did not extinguish debate over the legitimacy of exclusion of entire categories of people from citizenship rights. The debates were joined by educated leaders in the colonies and a few politicians in metropoles who took ideals of citizenship seriously.

The point, then, is that citizenship over the course of the nineteenth century—in Europe and beyond—did not become an agreed-upon concept that entailed an accepted set of rights and obligations in a defined space. It was a framework for debate over who could enjoy its fruits, who could be excluded, and what kind of polity people in different geographic and political locations could envision. The volatility of the debate was conditioned by the variety of political systems that existed simultaneously and increasingly rapid systems of long-distance communication. The world in the early twentieth century did not consist of equivalent political units. Within each imperial formation different categories of people had varying statuses, relations with the state, and relations—often tense—with each other. Imperial states—France and Great Britain as well as the Ottoman and Austro-Hungarian empires—depended in their rivalry with each other on the acquiescence and often the fighting capacity of subordinate elites, citizens, and subjects. They faced challenges from within as well as from outside. Many people became aware that others had rights that they themselves did not possess.

CHAPTER THREE

Empires, Nations, and Citizenship in the Twentieth Century

WRITING IN THE AFTERMATH of World War II and the Shoah, Hannah Arendt captured the power of citizenship by pointing to its negation. By stripping Jews of German citizenship the Nazis made them nonpersons in the global territorial order, setting the stage for the destruction of a people.[1]

Jurists and statesmen have recoiled at the notion of the stateless individual, the *apatride*. International refugees are considered a serious problem because of the liminal position of the refugee between his or her host country and country of origin. Persons displaced within their own countries, who are often numerous and living in appalling conditions, do not produce the same anxieties. Jurists and politicians seem convinced that every person belongs somewhere, and that somewhere is defined in an equivalent way throughout the world, as citizenship in a state.

What kind of state? What meaning does citizenship have when migration and mixing mean that state borders and linguistic or cultural affinity rarely correspond one-to-one, whatever the fiction in play? The conventional narrative of "empire to nation-state" obscures the varied transformations of citizenship in the twentieth century. New forms of empire (the USSR, the Nazis) with widely varying concepts of citizenship appeared even as some of the old ones (Austria-Hungary) were destroyed. Efforts to claim the rights of the citizen within colonial empires existed alongside attempts to seek independence. Although the loss of overseas empires left some western European states more focused on their existence as national political entities, by the 1990s they were looking toward a common European citizenship whose significance had to be worked out.

Citizenship has unquestionably been an important claim-making construct at the level of territorial states—claims for protection against enemy states and against the ravages of disease, old age, and, indeed, of global capitalism. It has been a framework in which people articulate their sense of commonality, with varying degrees of exclusionary and inclusionary sentiments. But the territorial state is not the only form of political belonging on which such aspirations have been focused, and it is not clear that the gains of social citizenship achieved within national frameworks can be defended in the current economic conjuncture.

In this chapter I will look at citizenship at different levels of inclusion, the *imperial* level among them. Sometimes an overarching citizenship was superposed on national citizenships: the British Commonwealth in 1948, the USSR in 1917, the Russian Federation in 1991, the European Union in 1993. I will also look in the opposite direction, at citizenship *within* a state, what theorists call group-differentiated citizenship or multinational citizenship, something that actually existed and exists today in India. A variant of differentiated citizenship—permitting people to be citizens in different ways—existed for a time in the country most associated with a unitary conception of citizenship, France.

Claims to make state correspond to nation include both colonized peoples' quest for liberation and dominant groups' efforts to purify a space via ethnic cleansing. The dissolution of empires—Ottoman, British, Soviet—did not end conflict over belonging and boundaries. Both world wars of the twentieth century ended with massive, coerced population transfers, the "unmixing of peoples."[2] Political movements have both sought to homogenize populations and to organize diversity. In either case, they confront not just cultural difference per se, but the relationship of difference and inequality—within nation-states, between metropoles and colonies, and among independent states. Poverty and violence send people across borders while others try to defend the boundaries of their supposed civilizations; we are still observing, long after Hannah Arendt wrote, the suffering of people who fall in between.

I ended the last chapter around the time of World War I. Old empires—Ottoman, Austro-Hungarian, Russian—had been troubled, yet during the war their citizens, as much as any, fought loyally and often effectively for them. The Ottomans, with help from the Germans, held off British, French, French African, Australian, New Zealander, and other troops at the Dardanelles and gave the British—who were largely using Indian troops—a tough fight in Basra and Mesopotamia. The downfall of the Ottoman and Austro-Hungarian empires came from choosing what became the losing side in a clash of empires. The Russian Empire couldn't defeat the onslaught of the German one, but a new variant on Russian empire arose from the debacle, with its own variant on imperial citizenship.

After the war the victors tried to encode new principles of relations among states, but the very act of imperial states imposing the nation-state form on the dismembered parts of losing empires was neither logically consistent nor politically viable. By insisting that the new states of eastern and central Europe corresponded to "nations" but that "minorities" in these states (although not in the territories of the great powers) had to be protected, the dominant powers exposed the poor fit between the newly created citizenships and the actual distribution of people over space. Self-determination, massive expulsions, and the notion of the "minority" were inextricably linked in the politics of Europe, while the League of Nation's mandate system added a gloss of trans-empire paternalism to the continued power of colonial states over subjects who could, under the new order, be legitimately excluded from citizenship until the ruling power decided otherwise.[3] In the ensuing years, some people would strive to push others into the situation of the second-class citizen or exclude them altogether from the polity, while others would demand the full rights of the citizen, whether in an empire that had relegated them to inferior status or in a state that they could label "their own."

Claiming and Bestowing Citizenship in the British Empire

In 1914, people were British in different ways. In the dominions —Canada, Australia, New Zealand, and South Africa—citizens governed themselves in most respects. The king, nevertheless, declared war on their behalf, although they had the choice of how to fight it. Appeals in legal cases from the dominions could go to the Privy Council in London, and symbols of royal rule not only abounded, but were taken seriously. Although the British government claimed that its subjects had rights anywhere in the empire, it would not interfere with the dominions' rights to govern themselves—and therefore to exclude British Indians from entry as well as treat their indigenous populations as they saw fit. Indians fought for the empire in large numbers, against the Germans as well as the Ottomans. Africans were recruited with varying degrees of coercion and relegated to porterage or other logistic operations, during which they were fed and treated badly and suffered high mortality from disease.

It was in relation to India that the problem of citizenship and empire was posed with the most immediacy. Indians could enter the United Kingdom, reside there, and even run (and occasionally be elected) for office. But Indians in India had no such status. They had minimal voice in public affairs and faced limits on assembly and speech.[4] In classic imperial style, Britain governed India in different ways: through the nominal sovereignty of indigenous elites in the princely states, more directly in other regions. The administrations differentiated people by religion and caste, by designation of certain peoples as "backward tribes" or "backward castes." The imperial rulers' relationship to the ruled was arranged into horizontal—and racialized—strata as well as vertical linkages through Indian elites.

Citizenship, in such a structure, was an important category of claim-making. Indian activists could pose their demands in both an imperial framework—on the empire as a whole—and a colonial one—within India—for political voice, social justice, and resources for particular castes or tribes.[5] From the mid-nineteenth century, the claim to political rights went along with economic and social complaints, first against the "drain" of Indian resources characteristic of an imperial economy, later for a living wage, for free education, for social recognition and material resources for the most subordinated elements of the class structure, for economic planning and redistribution, for redefining the status and role of women within Indian society.[6] Claim-making—in localities and in India as a whole— drew on an intense associational life, active journalism despite censorship, and incessant demands from labor, women's organizations, and others for social reform.[7]

No less a figure than Mohandas Gandhi invoked the notion of imperial citizenship to urge his followers to support the war effort of the British Empire (chapter 2). Political mobilization by the Indian National Congress escalated when Britain reneged on the promises it had made during World War I.[8] Imperial citizenship became a less appealing claim in the 1920s when the "white" dominions used their autonomous law-making capacity to exclude Indians from entering their territories, negating the right to mobility within the empire that Great Britain had appeared to offer. The South African leader Jan Smuts insisted, "There is no common equal British citizenship in the Empire, and it is quite wrong for a British subject to claim equal rights in any part of the Empire to which he has migrated or where he happens to be living."[9] That the British government acceded to arguments like this—as well as its failure to give Indians a serious role in the governing of India—led the Indian National Congress, after long and intense debates, to shift by 1929 from claiming more political power within the British Empire, through variants on imperial federalism, toward making independence the ultimate goal. Congress's reorientation was not just an instance of nationalism taking its inevitable course toward the nation-state. In Sunil Amrith's empire-wide perspective, "visions of imperial citizenship foundered on the shoals of white supremacy."[10]

Activists not only had to confront British power by deploying the language of rights and liberalism, but find common ground across a space differentiated by religion, communal affiliation, gender, and social status.[11] "Group-differentiated citizenship" emerged out of the differentiations of empire politics as politicians positioned themselves for independence. Mobilizing followers by social category became a way for politicians from the relatively deprived categories—the *dalit* leader B. R. Ambedkar most prominent among them—to make demands for "their" people. Socially minded elites envisioned reforming India by leveling upward, providing opportunities and recognition to those categories. Alongside the insistence within Indian political discourse, by the 1940s, on the need for "development" and for building a more equitable society, group differentiation encouraged a politics of patronage and of redistribution that reinforced rather than attenuated the particularistic structure of Indian society. Group-differentiated citizenship, after considerable controversy, was inscribed in the Indian constitution of 1950 and underlies the mobilization strategies of political parties to this day.

Controversy raged over including in the Indian constitution mention of social and economic rights—to education, to a minimum level of subsistence, to equality across gender and caste. While most participants in the constitutional debates in India advocated some form of social justice, they disagreed over whether social rights should be distinguished from the more readily justiciable civil and political rights. Was citizenship a sufficient end in itself for constitutional creation, providing the means by which a wider array of rights could be claimed in the future, or should the community express its ultimate goals from the start? In the end, writes Niraja Gopal Jayal, social rights in India remained the "poor cousins of civil and political rights." Scholars now lament the weakness of a "civic community" at the level of the nation as a whole.[12]

Citizenship in India emerged under the shadow of the violent partition that separated it from Pakistan.[13] Initially, Indian leaders leaned toward *jus soli*, with protections for "minority citizens," but in the frenzy of violence in August 1947 against Muslims in India and Hindus in Pakistan, citizenship legislation took a turn toward the defense of one's own kind. India wanted to prevent Muslims who had fled India in panic from returning after calm was restored, restricted their ability to claim property they had abandoned, and—a notable violation of citizenship norms elsewhere in the world—refused them access to courts in order to contest these exclusions. Pakistan did likewise. Both countries ended up with something more like *jus sanguinis*, defining inclusion and exclusion in religious terms and seeking to attract people in the diasporas back to their respective countries. During another period of violence leading up to the secession of East Pakistan from Pakistan in 1971 (creating the new country of Bangladesh), another wave of Muslim refugees trying to enter India reinforced this exclusionary trend in citizenship. "Inflexible citizenship" is how Joya Chatterji characterizes what emerged out of the quite different intentions of Indian and Pakistani leaders at the end of British rule.[14]

At first glance, group recognition in India seems to offer an historical example of the kind of multinational citizenship that scholars like Will Kymlicka advocate for the future (see the introduction). The example is not a particularly comforting one, for it underscores the pressures for group closure and for clientage that come with linking power and resources to collectivities that emphasize their particularistic basis. The dynamics of group-differentiated citizenship, however, are different in the two contexts. Kymlicka takes as his starting point the civic, democratic constitution of a territorial state, and he seeks the means to provide recognition within it for particular collectivities. Group differentiation in India, in contrast, came out of socially and religiously constituted categories, whose groupness was reinforced by colonial administration. On top of these collectivities, nationalists sought to turn the common ground that the Raj had defined into a fully constituted nation. This national sensibility built on common symbols and structures, but also a legacy of conflict and partition. Juxtaposing political theory and Indian practice emphasizes the difficulty of the question over which theorists have agonized: can one recognize cultural particularity or transcend it while still insisting upon the importance of shared, democratic, inclusive values?[15]

Trajectories out of the British Empire have been as varied as the forms of governing different peoples within it.[16] The British government learned the lesson of its heavy-handed actions that had precipitated the secession of the thirteen North American colonies in 1776, but the process of devolving power to the "white" dominions played out over more than a century. The ending of Privy Council appeals by citizens of Canada, Australia, and other dominions, as well as the partial suppression of British monarchal symbolism, only took place (and only partially) when the rest of the empire was being "decolonized."[17]

The British pattern of giving colonial governors considerable latitude to conduct administration through structures and political relationships specific to their territory channeled political mobilization to demands for voice within territorial institutions. Territorial administration provided concrete, and by the 1950s attainable, goals to political movements, which came to focus on turning the colony into a self-governing, nationally constituted state. The British government tried at times to attenuate the fragmenting tendencies of its imperial politics by organizing—on a top-down basis—federations in parts of the empire, in Central and East Africa and Malaya for example. The Malayan Federation was the most fully realized, giving rise to the relatively plural state of Malaysia, but not before the repression of a bloody revolution with both ethnic and class elements. The Central African Federation failed because what the government claimed was a structure intended to facilitate economic modernization was perceived—quite correctly—by African nationalists as a ploy to extend the power of white settlers. The East African community, never actually a federation, gave rise after the independence of its constituent states (Kenya, Tanzania, and Uganda) to valiant attempts at creating common markets and infrastructure, but foundered on the unequal geographic distribution of resources as well as disagreements among ruling elites over modes of governance and the territorial basis of each leader's support.

Alongside all of this came a final British attempt to make the Commonwealth into a meaningful institution. In the twilight of empire, one of the most far-reaching elements of that effort was the attempt to create a post-imperial citizenship, "post" in its roots in imperial citizenship.

In both world wars, the empire had been crucial to the survival of Great Britain, thanks to the enormous contributions of dominions, India, and the colonies. British leaders were conscious after the war that they might need such cooperation again and that Commonwealth territories now had more choice in the matter. When, beginning in 1946, Canada, Australia, and other dominions enacted legislation to define their own nationalities, the British Parliament had to respond. The result was the Nationality Act of 1948. The act created the overlapping statuses of "Commonwealth Citizen" and "Citizen of the United Kingdom and Colonies" alongside that of "British Subject." In the case of the dominions, it would be up to each to decide who was a national of Canada, Australia, or another dominion, and that nationality would automatically confer Commonwealth citizenship. Concerned in a time of challenge to empire to avoid accusations of racism, Parliament insured that its subjects in the remaining colonies, including Africa and the West Indies, would become "citizens of the United Kingdom and the Colonies."[18]

Among the rights that this citizenship conveyed was the right to enter, settle in, and work in the British Isles themselves, although Britain could not force dominions to acknowledge such a right. When the passenger liner *Empire Windrush* docked in England shortly after passage of the Nationality Act carrying hundreds of West Indians, it unleashed a wave of anxiety about the arrival of what might be a stream of nonwhite people claiming rights as British citizens. But, as a matter of state policy, the logic of maintaining empire trumped the logic of race, and the people of British colonies now had the right to enter the United Kingdom. In the 1950s, a British Colonial Secretary could assert that the people of the empire "can say *Civis Britannicus sum*," an echo of the *Civis Romanus sum* of the Roman Empire. That so many people from the colonies would actually exercise their new right to install themselves in the United Kingdom was not anticipated by policy-makers, and added to the anxiety many in Great Britain had over nonwhite immigration. Despite mixed motives and misgivings, writes Randall Hansen, "The 1950s were the defining years in the development of multicultural Britain." The 1948 Act gave people from the colonies and dominions the opportunity to make claims as people who were in some sense British, even if not all people in Great Britain viewed citizens from overseas in such terms.[19]

By 1962—when there was no longer much of an empire to maintain—the Nationality Act began to be eroded. The gap between a legally inclusive post-imperial citizenship and discrimination and prejudice in practice widened, until the legal regime caught up with the more exclusionary practices. Restrictive immigration laws—with particular effect on people of

African and Asian origin—undermined the possibility of an inclusive Britain in which former subjects would have a place.[20]

As I will describe below, the Nationality Act of 1948 had parallels to the citizenship clauses of the French constitution of 1946 and the further concessions the French government later made to African leaders. These leaders wanted their own nationalities to be recognized while their inhabitants retained the "superposed" nationality of the French Republic and the Community. The British and French versions of superposed nationality point to the willingness of these two powers to develop some kind of post-imperial political relationship, that, while facilitating the economic and geopolitical interests of the ex-colonial power, conveyed juridically enforceable rights across the space of the former empire to their former subjects.

Citizenship from Tsarist Empire to the Russian Federation

Let us turn to a framework for citizenship quite different from that of the British, one recognizing diverse peoples as elements of a multi-ethnic polity without presuming that sovereignty came from the people or that citizens should govern the state. I am referring to the Russian Empire, the Union of Soviet Socialist Republics, and the Russian Federation. "The pragmatic recognition of the multicultural composition of the empire," writes Jane Burbank, "was explicit in imperial law."[21] Ethnic Russians were only one of the many peoples of the empire, Russian Orthodoxy only one of its recognized faiths. All subjects, including Russians, were the subordinates of the emperor. Relations of tsar to people were vertical, superior to inferior, not the horizontal common belonging of a citizenship regime. But horizontal conceptions were present in people's expectations that as members of an imperial community they all possessed rights to the tsar's protection and care.[22]

Civil and economic rights were allocated according to estate status (nobles, clergy, merchants, peasants), location, religion, work, and combinations of these attributes. Russian peasants did not have the same rights as Russian nobles; Lutherans had different civil rights from those of the Orthodox. The elites of incorporated regions served as imperial intermediaries; some entered the highest ranks of the central government. In the sixteenth century, the Russian Empire acquired a large Muslim population, and Muslim clerics, like Orthodox ones, were given administrative tasks. The government at times moved people around the empire; deportation was part of an imperial repertoire of controlling people. From the time of Peter the Great (1682–1725), the tsarist regime, eager for taxes and recruits, instructed Orthodox priests to keep registers of births and deaths; by the nineteenth century, Catholic priests, Protestant pastors, rabbis, and imams were under similar instructions. Unlike the French *état civil* (chapter 2), the various registers and official documents of the tsarist regime recorded distinctions of status, religion, and ethnicity until the reforms of 1905–6. During the brief period of quasi-parliamentary rule after that date, reformers sought to erode the importance of estates and underline a direct relationship of individual and state institutions. But classification by "nationality"—Russian, Jewish, Tatar, Polish—remained in the registers and continued to be of importance in Soviet times.[23]

In the late nineteenth century, aware of the "civilizing missions" of other imperial powers, the tsarist government promoted Russifying policies, resettled Russian peasants to the east, and encouraged conversion to Orthodoxy. But a thoroughgoing nationalizing policy was not possible; effective governance over the widely dispersed, differentiated population required the accommodation of local elites. Eric Lohr refers to the politics of "separate deals."[24] Poles and Jews were particularly problematic populations, whose rights were adjusted several times in the nineteenth and early twentieth centuries. The Russian state was for a long time cautious about extending formal citizenship rights to foreigners, but increasingly interested in establishing commercial relationships with them. At the same time, the state wanted to hold onto its people and put obstacles in the way of subjects who tried to emigrate.[25]

The Russian word for "citizenship," *grazhdanstvo*, like its Latin and Germanic equivalents, has roots in terms for "city." In the nineteenth century liberal and radical critics of the autocracy used the term, demanding equal rights for the whole population and referring to alleged western European norms. They confronted Russia's version of a rights regime: rights handed down by the tsar and adhering to particular categories of people. Those rights were less than inalienable but more than arbitrary, and the differentiation among the tsar's subjects did not make them less members of the polity.[26] Differentiated citizenship set out a field of political action in late-nineteenth- and early-twentieth-century Russia. Some political figures advocated equality; others maneuvered to promote "their" people's rights within the differentiated system; and still others worked for a revolution that would bring in an entirely new order.[27]

After the revolution of February 1917 overthrew the Romanov dynasty, reformers in the Provisional Government called for "full 'citizenship,' defined as equal rights and obligations before the law for all individual members of the polity."[28] Eight months later the Bolsheviks went back to a citizenship that put more emphasis on the "obligation" side of the equation than the "rights" side. Citizenship in the new Communist state was once again differentiated, this time by another kind of status: "worker" or "peasant" as opposed to "bourgeois" or "noble."[29]

A major innovation of the Soviet regime—also building on the imperial past—was the creation of national republics.[30] Each was built around a predominant ethnic group. Each would have its own nationality, based on that of the most populous group in the region. The leadership of each republic would come from this dominant ethnic group, mobilized through the Communist Party. The catalogue of nationalities and borders was not fixed, but a politically charged issue. Citizenship of the USSR, like the post-imperial citizenships of France and Great Britain, was superposed on national citizenships.[31] The significance of citizenship—especially the obligations that went along with the rights—was shaped by the centralizing, revolutionary politics of the Party. Although political rights were minimal, social rights were substantial, not least the right to education. These rights were also allocated in differentiated ways according to class, ethnicity, and place in the party hierarchy.[32]

The collapse of the Soviet Union in 1991 meant the reallocation of Soviet citizens among the fifteen successor states. It also meant the loosening of controls on emigration and foreign travel, as well as the opening up of "closed" cities. The picture was complicated by the presence of numerous people in territories that did not correspond to their nationality, both Russians in the newly independent states and non-Russians in the Russian Federation.[33] For a time, the Russian Federation simplified procedures for former Soviet citizens to acquire Russian nationality or to hold dual citizenship, but after 2000 the regime became more restrictive.[34] The Russian Federation, true to its name, remained a multinational polity that recognized ethnic and religious particularity through its territorial subdivision into eighty-five components of varying status. Thirty-five different languages are used in administration. The tension between centralizing control and recognition of diversity is a dynamic element in today's Russian Federation.

Citizenship in the Post-Ottoman Middle East

Although the Ottoman Empire collapsed in the same cataclysm that brought down the tsarist empire, the fate of its citizens took different turns. As late as 1910–11, the possibility that Ottoman citizenship had a place not just for Turks but for Arabs, Greeks, Jews, and others was still alive, even if it was becoming increasingly problematic by virtue of the ascendency of a self-consciously Turkish elite to power. The Balkan Wars, the Armenian genocide, defeat in World War I, the Versailles treaty and the forced breakup of the Ottoman Empire, the struggle that gave rise to the Turkish state, and the forced migrations of Turks and Greeks to "their" respective states violently transformed the relationship of people to space. Post-Ottoman state boundaries were not indigenous creations but impositions of the imperial powers that emerged victorious in World War I.[35] The ways in which peoples were allocated to states in these years has bedeviled the region to this day.

Part of the process was supposed to be supervised by international organizations, but the League of Nations and its Permanent Mandates Commission represented more the internationalization of colonialism than the universalization of citizenship.[36] Part of the Ottoman territories were divided between France and Britain, and the unequal conflict between two rival "national" claims to Israel-Palestine has been a part of world history ever since, as have the communal conflicts within the newly constructed states of Syria, Lebanon, and

Iraq. The mandatory powers did their best—with considerable violence—to avoid the mobilization of populations in these territories, a policy that has not helped to produce a basis for democratic politics or respect for civic rights. Kurds and Palestinians have yet to find a place within the allocation of citizenships, and face serious discrimination in whatever state they find themselves. Both social and religious fragmentation within Middle Eastern countries and memories of past unity under Islamic empires compromise the sense of common purpose of citizenship in the actually existing states. Anti-imperialism, anti-Zionism, and a rather ill-defined pan-Arabism or pan-Islamism have had durable influence in the region, while neither national projects nor some kind of supranational institutions have had sustained traction. The harshness of current global economic relations and the lack of opportunities for upward mobility within national societies adds to the strains. Young men become available for various purposes, from migration to support their families to fighting for the Islamic State.

Sally Cummings and Raymond Hinnebusch contrast the compromised sovereignties of the Middle East with the countries of Central Asia that emerged after 1991 out of the imperial cauldron of tsarist Russia and the Soviet Union and where Islam, albeit in different forms, is also the most important religious affiliation. The two regions share a political style that is personalistic and clientelistic, with little place for legitimate opposition or respect for the civil rights of citizens, but the Central Asian provinces were integrated into a Soviet project that was more "real and meaningful"—with important investments in education and industrialization—than the supposedly liberal policies of European powers in the Middle East. The very lack of a liberal democratic ideal may have enabled the compromises between Moscow and provincial capitals that facilitated both the Soviet regime in the region and the relatively smooth devolution of most of its territories into formal sovereignties with pragmatic relations with Russia and decidedly illiberal governance.[37]

Subjects, Citizens, and Foreigners: A French Empire Story

Most French people today see their history since 1789 at the opposite end of the spectrum from the histories just described: an "indivisible" republic, in which all citizens have the same rights. Contrary to images of France as a unitary polity moving through time, I will argue that as late as the 1950s, the possibility of an imperial or post-imperial citizenship, incorporative but differentiated, and the possibility of turning empire into federation or confederation were at the core of political interaction and contention between France and its African territories.

The empire in the early and mid-twentieth century was not neatly divided between metropole and colony, its people between citizens and subjects. It consisted of European France; the "old colonies," such as Martinique and Réunion, where inhabitants including the slaves freed in 1848 were citizens; "new colonies," notably those of sub-Saharan Africa, where the large majority were considered subjects; Algeria, whose territory was considered an integral part of the French Republic but whose population was divided between settlers, with citizenship rights, and indigenous people, mostly Muslims, who were relegated to the category of subject; protectorates, such as Morocco, Tunisia, and most of Indochina, which were in reality governed by France but formally remained sovereign states with their own nationalities; and (after 1919) former German colonies and Ottoman provinces, mandated to France by the League of Nations and to be governed like colonies but with the presumption that they would eventually develop their own nationalities. In the Quatre Communes of Senegal, original inhabitants had the rights of the citizen without having to give up their civil status as Muslims (chapter 2). In other territories indigenous people who gave up their personal status under Islamic or "customary" law and convinced administrators that they had adopted a French way of life could in principle acquire citizenship. Children of mixed parentage, usually of a citizen father and an indigenous mother, would be citizens if the father recognized his offspring or if the mother or a charitable institution could convince authorities that the child was being brought up in a suitably French manner.[38] These narrow passages to citizenship allowed French elites to assert that they adhered to republican ideals while maintaining exclusionary and demeaning practices.

Political movements in Algeria, Indochina, and sub-Saharan Africa focused initially on claiming the full rights of the French citizen. World War I reinforced such claims, for soldiers from across the empire fought and died in the trenches, sharing in a common imperial cause but experiencing racial discrimination in many ways. After the war, leaders in the colonies could assert that their constituents had paid the "blood tax."

No less a figure than Georges Clemenceau—the wartime prime minister—argued that Algerians' participation in the war entitled them to become French citizens without giving up their Muslim status. He was in part agreeing with the program of the Algerian political activist known as Emir Khaled calling for citizenship without change of personal status, representation in the Assemblée Nationale, the end of repressive laws, and access to the civil service.[39] Meanwhile, influential settlers in Algeria, who possessed the status of the citizen, were arguing that they—but not Muslim Algerians—should not only have full citizenship rights, but also have autonomous authority within Algeria. That demand was intended to insure that a more liberal French government would not, one day, grant Muslim Algerians more rights, and it echoed the demands made by French planters in Saint Domingue in 1789 for both citizenship and autonomy, so that they could keep slaves in their place.[40] The government met neither demand.

The political activism of colonial subjects led to a reaction on the part of colonial administrators. In the 1920s, many of them were insisting that citizenship would not be good for Africans and that their progress should occur within their own cultural milieu. This politics of retraditionalization paralleled British colonial policies in Africa, where political ferment and claims to imperial citizenship were countered by an effort to stuff Africans back into tribal containers. Among Muslim Algerians, a variety of claims emerged: for identification with the Muslim world, for recognition of an Algerian nation within the French Empire—or potentially outside it.[41] Aimé Césaire, poet and politician from Martinique, could simultaneously assert that the descendants of slaves who made up the majority of the population of the Caribbean islands shared a cultural connection to Africa—*négritude*, he called it—and insist on full rights as French citizens and for their territory's status to be changed from "colony" to "department," equivalent to that of the political units of metropolitan France. His ally in the *négritude* movement, Léopold Sédar Senghor of Senegal, also combined a militant assertion of the value of African civilization—alongside and equivalent to European civilization—with a demand for the rights of the citizen for France's African subjects.[42]

Those rights had been systematically denied. During the war, both the Vichy regime that ruled most of France's colonies and the Free French who managed to control French Equatorial Africa paid little attention to previous concerns about subjecting noncitizens to forced labor. Deadly incidents of state violence at war's end—at Sétif in Algeria and Thiaroye in Senegal, and later in Madagascar—suggested that the repressive might of colonial regimes would continue to be deployed against a variety of challenges. What changed the situation was the postwar government's realization of its weakness and the need to reconfigure the complex structure of empire if France were to remain something more than a small state on the western fringe of Eurasia.

Devastated by its defeat by Germany in 1940 and its loss of effective control over its most lucrative overseas possession, Indochina, to the Japanese, France founded a new republic, the Fourth. The question of whether a republic could insist that around half of its people were "French" but not citizens resurfaced in a way that reminded some of the debates over citizenship in the colonies that began in 1789. France had to write a new constitution for the new Republic, and that process meant that the future of empire had to be openly debated.

The government began with a name change: the French Empire became the French Union and colonies overseas territories. The government accepted that representatives of the diverse peoples of the empire—including subjects—would have a voice in writing the constitution, but not in proportion to their numbers. The presence of even a small number of overseas deputies—Senghor and Césaire among them—insured that the most profound problems of citizenship in a diverse and unequal polity had to be confronted directly.[43]

One side in the debates over the constitution insisted that France could only be a great power if it were an ensemble of diverse and equal people. Others worried that France might become "the colony of its former colonies," given the larger overseas population compounded by the perception that the Union's subjects were ill-educated and lacked the historical connections and common culture of people who were genuinely French. Such considerations recall the anxieties that had emerged in the debates in the Spanish Empire over the constitution of 1812 (chapter 2). The starting point of the debate in 1946 was the notion that France was an assemblage of peoples, and the relationship of its components could be altered in the interest of preserving the whole.

Conscious of the imperial context, deputies evoked in their debates the edict of Caracalla of AD 212 (chapter 1), interpreting it as conferring citizenship on the entire Roman Empire (except, to be sure, women and slaves) without making them give up their diverse civilizations. Other imperial precedents were cited—the Austro-Hungarian Empire, the Ottomans—and federal precedents as well—the United States, Switzerland, and, even by non-Communist deputies, the system of national republics of the USSR.

In September 1946, overseas deputies argued vociferously to put citizenship rights into the constitution, and at one point boycotted the assembly to demonstrate that the new republic would have no legitimacy overseas if their demands were not met. The wiser heads in the government realized that the acquiescence, at least, of the overseas deputies, however small their numbers, was politically necessary. In the end, the institutions of the French Union created by the constitution were compromises. They kept the real power in Paris, leaving advocates of a post-imperial federalism—entailing autonomy for territories within the larger federation—in the lurch. But Senghor, Césaire, and their colleagues won their minimum demand. The inhabitants of the overseas territories became citizens. Moreover, they did not have to give up their personal status under Islamic or "customary" law. Marriage, inheritance, and filiation—in overseas but not in European France—did not have to come under the civil code. A Muslim man could have more than one wife, vote in an election for the French legislature, and seek a place in a French university or the French civil service. The personal status clause implied recognition of cultural diversity, even if it at times compromised principles of equality—particularly gender equality—in the French Republic.[44] The protectorates, such as Tunisia, possessed their own nationalities and thus had a special citizenship status of uncertain significance—as citizens of the French Union—created for them.[45] But the inhabitants of Senegal, Côte d'Ivoire, and Algeria became citizens of the French Republic.

What this would mean was still subject to the differentiated and contested practices characteristic of imperial polities. The "old colonies" like Martinique achieved the recognition Aimé Césaire had sought for them. They became French departments.[46] In Algeria, the settler lobby and allies in the French military, business, and political establishment strove to subvert the constitution's more inclusive intentions. They insured that European settlers, voting in a separate electoral college, would continue to possess political power disproportionate to their number, leaving Muslim Algerians with second-class citizenship and pushing Algeria down a road to violent conflict.[47]

In sub-Saharan Africa, it took ten years to achieve universal suffrage and territorial legislatures with real power. But citizenship there quickly became a claim-making construct: claims for recognition of France's diversity, for economic and social equality, and for remedying the shortcomings of the constitution. Trade unions pressed for equal pay for equal work and a labor code based on the metropolitan version, a goal African leaders achieved in 1952.

Unlike in the time of Caracalla, citizenship was now hitched to the welfare state, to new norms concerning labor, and to the state's responsibility for the standard of living of the polity as a whole.[48] France could no longer neatly segregate its overseas citizens from the social attributes of citizenship. By the mid-1950s, the costs of imperial citizenship were escalating.

Senghor sought to push political reform toward the creation of a layered form of sovereignty: each territory would choose a government with authority over local affairs; French West Africa as a whole would constitute an African federation with a legislature and executive; and this federation would associate with other territories and federations in a reformed French Union in which all inhabitants would be rights-bearing citizens. Basic rights would be guaranteed at the Union level, making them both portable as people exercised their freedom of movement around the Union and insulated from ambitious politicians at the territorial level. The French Union would limit its actions to foreign affairs, defense, development, and other agreed-upon domains and become a confederation, recognizing the national personality of its component parts. Senghor saw nationality not in terms of Senegalese or Ivorians but of Africans, or at least those Africans who shared the French language and the experience of French institutions.

The layering of sovereignty was for Senghor a way of confronting a basic problem that the nationalists of his era and commentators on nationalism of a subsequent time have had trouble dealing with: the theoretical equality among sovereign states and their actual inequality. Senghor called for a combination of two forms of solidarity: "horizontal," of Africans with each other within and across the territories making up the continent, and "vertical," of Africans with France, whose superior material resources, educational levels, technical capacities, and experiences with democratic politics had something to offer to Africans. Recognizing inequality was the only way of combating it—as long as Africans could demand equality from a position of strength.

Other African leaders wanted to bypass the West African federation while favoring direct membership of each territory in a Franco-African Community.[49] Such possibilities were being debated in Africa as the French government came to realize that it was caught in a trap between following through on the logic of citizenship—which was costly—and the risk of a cycle of rebellion and repression, like that it faced in Algeria, now taking place under the gaze of international institutions and observers who did not see colonial rule as inevitable. The only way to get African leaders to back off their demands for economic and social equality was to give them ever more autonomy in governing themselves.

When the French government in 1958 offered each territory the option of immediate independence or continued participation with a large measure of self-government as Member States of a revised French Community, only Guinea voted for immediate and complete independence. After initial reluctance, the French government accepted demands from African Member States that the Community recognize the right of each state to define its own nationality, which would automatically confer the "superposed nationality" of the French Republic and of the Community. Here is what scholars today call multilevel citizenship.[50]

But African leaders could not agree on whether or how to federate among themselves, and France was anxious to avoid the obligations of too close a union. Africa's leading politicians came to believe that bilateral relations of sovereign states with France corresponded better to the contingencies of the moment than did layered sovereignty. For a time it looked as if four French West African territories would unite in an African federation, but in the end only two, Senegal and the Sudan, joined up, seriously compromising its chances of success.[51] The new entity was named the Mali Federation after an ancient African empire. It got as far as writing a constitution, briefly governing itself within the French Community, and successfully negotiating with France for independence as a single state. But two months after independence, as Senegalese and Sudanese leaders feared that each was encroaching on the other's political base, the federation broke up in anger and Senegal and the Sudan went their separate ways (the latter claiming the name of Mali, but as Republic, not Federation). Still, it was only in 1960 that the dissolution of the French Empire in sub-Saharan Africa into territorial nation-states became the only exit option.

Even then, the separation of citizenships implicit in the end of colonial rule was attenuated by bilateral agreements. The French government at the time was more worried that French citizens who wanted to do business, reside in, or possess property in former colonies would become mere foreigners and that their property could be in jeopardy than that former citizens of overseas territories might migrate to France. That France, in the midst of an economic boom, needed labor made the government all the more willing to see its former citizens come to its places of work. The independence treaties conveyed reciprocal rights similar to those previously conveyed by common citizenship, minus political rights but including the right of former citizens to enter and reside in France and current French citizens to do likewise in former colonies. Moreover, the French government decided that anyone born a citizen before the date of independence of a former overseas territory could have his or her French nationality recognized—as opposed to applying for naturalization—as long as the individual established residence within the current boundaries of the French Republic. France even went so far as to change its constitution to allow a former territory to remain a Member State of the Community after becoming independent. In actuality, the Community was no longer a functioning entity, but the episode reveals the desperation of the French government to bind former citizens—if no longer its colonial territories—to itself. It was for a time extending to its former citizens one of the most important rights they had won in 1946: to enter, reside in, and seek education or employment in European France.

Treaties can be abrogated and laws changed more easily than constitutions. When the French government, in 1974, decided to move to a more restrictive citizenship regime, there were no more Africans in its political institutions and the decision was its to make. The new laws cut off immigration of workers and wound down the special regime to which its former overseas citizens were entitled, although it allowed properly documented citizens to bring in certain categories of relatives.

The new laws defined a gap—indeed a canyon—between people entitled to the security and benefits of French citizenship and people who were present in France, often at work, without legal authority. Those people began to call themselves the "sans papiers," the undocumented.[52] The separation of citizenships encouraged many French people to insist that there was a basic distinction between "Français de souche," French people who claim the historical heritage of Frenchness, and others, including people with proper citizenship status but marked as "issus de l'immigration," coming from immigration. Such a distinction is behind the development of a xenophobic far right in France. But among defenders of French republican and egalitarian traditions, many insist that equality among citizens means that there is only one way to be French, and anybody who does not conform to those (not entirely clear) expectations was guilty of "communitarianism" and endangered the coherence of the Republic.[53] What is easily forgotten is that the French constitution of 1946 (and its successor of 1958) specified in its personal status clause that one could be French in more than one way.

The constitution of 1946 was not the result of a more generous, inclusive sentiment among French people, but reflected reasons of state. France was trying to hold together what it had once called an empire, then a Union, later a Community. Once France gave up its empire, those reasons of state no longer applied.[54] In this context, the myth of an unbroken line of French citizenship from 1789 to the present had its uses for different sides—for some to articulate a more national conception of the polity, for others to claim economic and social equality within the French nation. Nevertheless, that so many actors from 1945 to 1960—African and French—tried to find new formulas for preserving an inclusive citizenship in a diverse and unequal political body is a lesson worth remembering in a world that remains diverse and unequal.[55]

Citizenship and the Nation-State in Post-Imperial Africa

And what of citizenship in Africa after the end of empire?[56] The picture is mixed. One side is the vigor with which some Africans have defended the citizen's right to a voice in politics. In 2012, when the incumbent president of Senegal, Abdoulaye Wade, tried to manipulate the electoral system to perpetuate his power—first by allowing himself to get around term limits to run for a third turn, then by fiddling the electoral rules in his favor—young people in Dakar and other cities took to the streets. Rap musicians played a key role in mobilizing youth. The demonstrations succeeded in blocking Wade's electoral manipulations and—to the surprise of some of my Senegalese friends—the elections turned out to be reasonably fair and resulted in Wade's defeat and the installation of Macky Sall as president.[57] A couple of years later, when Blaise Campaoré, president of Burkina Faso, tried to extend his 27 years in power, similar demonstrations erupted and Campaoré was forced to flee the country and new elections were held. An attempt by Campaoré's praetorian guard to restore him failed in the face of popular demonstrations led by organizations with names like *Balai citoyen* (citizen broom), *Citoyen africain pour la renaissance* (African citizen for the renaissance), and *Front de résistance citoyenne* (citizen resistance front).[58] In other countries as well there has been resurgence of political debate—in print, on radio talk shows, in "radio trottoir" (the street). Such debates have brought out both attachment to states as they exist today—to Uganda, to Kenya, to Benin—and insistence on the part of at least a portion of the public that the state respect the demands and expectations of its citizens.[59]

Claim-making in the name of citizenship—for political voice and fair elections, for equitable treatment of workers, for public services—does not necessarily triumph. The mobilization of citizens in African countries confronts not just the repressive power of the state but relationships that seem to offer more protection or opportunities than the collective action of citizens: poor people seeking wealthy patrons or people relying on the support of ethnic or religious communities.[60] It confronts as well a global economic order in which African states have limited means to fulfill the expectations of their citizens for a decent standard of living.

Citizenship in its national sense is not always an unmitigated blessing; it can be the basis of xenophobic politics as well as civic order. In South Africa, mobs of young men have beaten and sometimes killed immigrants from neighboring countries who were selling things on the street or seeking low-skilled work. The mobs proclaim the desire to keep jobs in

South Africa in the hands of South Africans. They do not recall the importance of regional connections in the struggle against apartheid. Such xenophobic behavior reflects, in this instance, the triumph of state-defined boundaries over webs of connection that at one time were important parts of people's lives.[61]

Similarly, the Côte d'Ivoire had long attracted migrants from a wide region, and it shared with the people of neighboring states a history of mobilization to make meaningful a common French citizenship.[62] But even while the debate over federation and confederation was ongoing in French West Africa, a pogrom took place in Abidjan in 1958, led by "native" Ivorians— and not the poorest among them—against workers from Dahomey and Togo who had "taken" jobs from local people.

The riot was an embarrassment to Félix Houphouët-Boigny, the leading politician from the Côte d'Ivoire. Although he opposed the African federation advocated by Senghor in favor of the direct participation of African territories in a French federation, Houphouët-Boigny did not take a narrow view of what political belonging meant in Africa. His career had taken off in 1944 when he organized an effort to ban forced labor in French Africa. It was people from the north of the Côte d'Ivoire or the neighboring French territories of Upper Volta, Sudan, and Niger who had been forcefully recruited to work for white planters in the fertile and well-watered southern Côte d'Ivoire. The end of forced labor liberated not only the laborers, but the African farmers of the coastal region, who now could get labor that had heretofore been reserved for whites. Coming to power with independence in 1960, Houphouët-Boigny understood quite well that the economic development of his territory depended on people from elsewhere in former French Africa. Moreover, in 1946 he had helped to found a political party (of which he remained president) with branches in every territory of French Africa, confronting the French government with an expression of African solidarity.

After his disappointment at not being able to enact the French federation that he sought, Houphouët-Boigny nonetheless tried to develop an inclusive version of Ivorian citizenship.[63] He wanted citizens of neighboring states whose leaders were his political allies to have the rights of the Ivorian citizen when they were within the country, giving up those rights when they left. Neither his own cadres nor the leaders of other states accepted his proposition; they had a narrower view of citizenship. But Houphouët-Boigny was a master at forging personal ties to the elites of different ethnic groups within his country's diverse population. He remained in power for 33 years. When he died in 1993, the vertical ties he created disappeared with him, and his successors lacked his ability and legitimacy and faced a situation where the export economy was in crisis and jobs were scarce.

As politicians from the northern region of Côte d'Ivoire contended for leadership, others tried to exclude them on the grounds that their parents were from neighboring states. Such was the fate of Alassane Ouattara, the leading opponent of the incumbent president. The exclusionary faction, eventually headed by President Laurent Gbagbo, talked of "ivoirité," the quality of being a genuine Ivorian, a truly autochthonous member of the Ivorian nation.[64] Tensions were high between citizens from the northern Côte d'Ivoire suspected of foreign origins and southerners who saw themselves as true Ivorians. The government tried to restrict "foreigners'" access to land. The crisis turned into a struggle for the state, degenerating into a civil war in 2011 when Gbagbo refused to accept the results of an election that had voted in Ouattara. The conflict ended when France and the association of West African states sent troops, who helped the militias of Ouattara and installed him in power. His presence reversed the exclusion of northerners from full Ivoirian citizenship, but not the tendency toward ethnic factionalism and favoritism.

Projecting a reified notion of the true citizen—Ivorian, Zambian, Tanzanian—and defining rivals as "foreign" is one way in which ruling elites used the resource of sovereignty to keep themselves in power. As Thandika Mkandawire astutely remarks, "The problem is not so much that the nationalists accepted existing colonial borders, but rather that this acceptance gave individual states carte blanche in terms of what they could do to their citizens within these borders."[65]

There are other ways to look at the citizenship question in Africa. Many observers, African and otherwise, believe that most Africans focus their sense of themselves and the relationships that provide access to the most basic resources through a primary attachment to communities defined by language, shared social practices, and a putative common history. To acquire land in much of Africa, for instance, the citizen often cannot simply act like an anonymous individual, pay his or her money, and expect courts or other state institutions to guarantee property. In rural areas, the individual may need to be an accepted community member to have access to land. "One first needs to be recognized as a 'son' or 'daughter' of a local community," writes Carola Lentz in reference to Ghana, and it is through such recognition that "one enjoys full rights over landed property and can legitimately partake in local political affairs."[66] She claims that only five percent of land in West Africa comes under the kind of regime of title documentation that state courts can readily enforce. Many claims to land are based on a "first-comer narrative," an historical claim of belonging to a community that was the "original" occupant of the land—a claim requiring witnesses and testimony and often entailing conflict. Such claim-making can be adaptable to economic incentives and political changes, and, Lentz argues, is not necessarily incompatible with agricultural development. But it assumes a particularistic pattern of belonging, with deep roots in local histories, that exists in tension with the formalized belonging that citizenship in a territorial state implies. Focusing land issues on local hierarchies can have important political consequences, as Catherine Boone points out: "By segmenting communities along communal lines and shoring up hierarchy within them, the neocustomary land regimes have also worked to containerize land politics in ethnic jurisdictions, tamp down the scale of politics, and reproduce ethnicity as the basis of politics."[67]

Particularly in the early years after independence, radical African leaders like Sékou Touré of Guinea and Modibo Keita of Mali viewed indigenous societies as feudal, dominated by chiefs who kept former slaves—and women more generally—in a state of voicelessness, subordination, and precarious access to land. Citizenship in a new nation promised liberation and equality. Their diagnosis was often to the point, their remedies not necessarily emancipatory. Many people from highly stratified societies took the task of liberation into their own hands by migrating to cities or neighboring countries.[68] In other contexts, elites defined the good citizen—who might be awarded accordingly—as one who supported the leader or the party, weaving citizenship and clientage into a single pattern.[69]

The ethnic fragmentation of African societies could make it easier for governing elites to defend their own power, as long as the cooperation of regional elites could be assured by a mixture of patronage and coercion. In South Africa, which has what many consider the world's most progressive constitution, the government has at times backed the power of chiefs in the areas that the previous, white-dominated regime had designated for

African settlement, conferring on them the power to allocate much of the land. In these instances "rural people are no longer considered to be rights-bearing citizens, with the capacity to enforce their land rights against the state and others." In other situations the government oscillates between conflicting imperatives: its desire to develop individual property ownership and "responsible" economic behavior by rural cultivators, its need to acknowledge the association that many South Africans make between the citizenship they acquired in 1994 and access to land, and the variability and complexity of power relations in different parts of the country. Citizenship in South Africa has not produced a unified, horizontal society, but a highly differentiated and unequal one.[70]

Within states, political actors try to draw on both "civic" ties—to the state, its institutions, and the national collectivity— and "traditional" ties—to villages, ethnic groups, kinship networks—in order to attach supporters to their cause. Political parties contesting elections call on a variety of social ties to mobilize voters—as they do in many parts of the world.[71] Some consider that such strategies accentuate "tribalism," but in any case politicians are working with social structure in all its complexity, not with an ideal type of the anonymous individual in relation to the state.

The idea of "belonging" in Africa before colonization did not necessarily mean that the continent was divided into distinct communities each of which was blessed with a strong sense of commonality and equality. Distinctions of gender, age, class, and status are as much part of African history as of any other.[72] Arguably, differentiation within communities has become starker over time: with growing population in many parts of rural Africa, more pressure on access to land, and scarce jobs, a vast number of people have more to demand from a small number of potential patrons with access to resources at both local and national levels. Such circumstances, even in instances of regular elections and relatively open media debate, place a higher premium on the vertical ties of patronage than on the horizontal notions of civic belonging, impartial rule of law, and equal political voice.[73]

It would be a mistake to consider a vision of citizenship that focuses on civic attachment to be the virtuous twin of ethnic citizenship. Both can be bounded and exclusionary or both can imply recognition of others' equivalent claims. Neither necessarily implies empathy toward people who fall in between categories, notably refugees. A lot depends on context.

Civic and ethnic citizenship can be in dynamic tension with each other. Juan Obarrio worries that the emergence of what he calls "customary citizenship" in Mozambique renders democracy incomplete. Coming to power in 1975, after a bitter and bloody struggle against the Portuguese colonial regime, the government tried in vain to suppress customary authority in the name of a unified, socialist citizenry. Having given up that battle, it now recognizes community courts that enforce the legal norms of particular ethnic groups, as articulated in many instances by "traditional" chiefs. Something like the ethnically defined colonial subject thus creeps back into the status of the Mozambican citizen. Elisio Macamo, in contrast, sees the problem in Mozambique less as the return of "customary" norms and authority than a combination of revolutionary arrogance and clientelism: the triumph of a liberation movement that saw its role as educating the populace rather than listening to it, and that insisted (even after losing its socialist fervor) on having its way, creating a "political culture which is deeply hostile to citizenship." Jason Hickel, meanwhile, sees the problem from a different angle. His studies in Zulu-speaking areas of South Africa suggest that many people see no place for themselves in the unitary, civic notion of citizenship preached for many years by the African National Congress. Instead, they place value on respect for elders, for local hierarchies, for maintenance of the kinship structure, for a gendered division of labor, all of which they see as "crucial to collective well-being." Hickel's goal is not to excuse anti-democratic practices, but to point to the powerful reasons why not everyone in Africa eagerly embraces the values of liberal democracy.[74] The question these accounts leave us with is whether conceptions of democratic and customary citizenship, of civic engagement and patron-client relations, are locked in a zero-sum game, or whether individual freedom, collective belonging, and hierarchical relationships can be reconciled. We are confronted not with an inherent characteristic of Africa, but with variations on a fundamental problem in studying citizenship.

Some scholars belittle the regularizing structures of elections and negotiations as European imports while celebrating patron-client relations—punctuated by the "unruly" intervention of popular classes—as means of making claims on the state. Patrons do distribute resources, and mass unrest can force governments to make concessions. But it is unlikely that patrons will continue to work for large numbers of clients if they are not disciplined in some way—by the prospect of being thrown out in an election for instance—and episodes of burning tires in the streets are unlikely to produce sustained results unless they are accompanied by the kind of "linear process of negotiation, deliberation and consensus seeking" that these authors seem to belittle.[75] The danger in relying on the politics of patronage, as Harri Englund puts it, is that "Under the conditions of rampant poverty and political turmoil, intermediate solidarities can quite as much support warlords as moral ethnicities."[76] If civic politics rarely dispenses with patronage relationships, patronage without civic politics can lead to the mobilization of strong-armed clienteles clashing with other clienteles, all the more dangerous when such collectivities follow ethnic lines.

We see here a new form of tensions that have long been part of the vitality of African societies, between kinship groups and kingdoms or empires, between attachment to locality and mobility, between attachment to local symbols and adherence to wider religious communities. The supposed intimacy of the "group" may conceal oppression and hierarchy, and the supposed egalitarianism of the civic may leave politics remote from lived experience and thereby encourage the communalism that the civic was supposed to avoid. Citizens' engagements with each other play out in a wide field, beyond state boundaries. Especially since World War II, Africans have migrated to many parts of the world seeking work, sometimes acquiring citizenship in host countries, but often retaining ties to their countries of origin and sending remittances "home" to sustain families, build houses and mosques, and contribute to government coffers—a diasporic citizenship in action.[77]

Whether such tensions lead to violent conflict or to oppressive state structures intended to suppress tensions or else to creative forms of federalism and attempts to balance different kinds of attachments is a question whose stakes are high. Ethiopia, for instance, adopted in 1995 a constitution that referred, using plurals, to "We, the Nations, Nationalities and Peoples of Ethiopia." Federation did not come about through the uniting of preexisting units, but followed a plan laid out by the central government. Of some 80 ethno-territorial units in Ethiopia, only six received the status of a "mother state." But the federal structure did give recognition to ethnic diversity and de-volved, for a time, significant power to provinces. Lahra Smith argues that the system was intended to produce "meaningful citizenship"—attuned to people's perception of themselves and to the importance of different collectivities making claims for resources on the federal state. It worked better in some regions than others, but the gestures toward decentralization were soon overwhelmed by the ruling elite's urge to do whatever neces-sary to remain in power, hence "rather familiar patterns of re-pression, authoritarianism, and narrowing of political space."[78]

A counterpoint to the trajectories of citizenship in post–World War II tropical Africa is the case of South Africa in the years 1948–94, when a white minority ruled over a heteroge-neous polity, denying people of African and Asian origin polit-ical voice and subjecting them to harsh policies of racial dis-crimination and exploitation, a policy known as apartheid (from the Afrikaans word for separate). Apartheid evolved into something of a caricature of the politics of citizenship in the decolonizing world. Earlier, South Africa's racial politics fell well within the spectrum of twentieth-century colonialism, with its invidious racial distinctions. In the late nineteenth cen-tury, tensions between the English- and Afrikaans-speaking white populations made it difficult for either to identify fully as "British" or "South African," but they could agree on distin-guishing themselves from indigenous people or South Asian immigrants.[79] "South African" came to mean "white South Af-rican." After achieving self-governing status within the British Commonwealth in 1910 and coming under control of a self-consciously Afrikaner political movement in 1948, South Africa took a different course from other British territories. South African elites turned white domination from an *imperial* into a *national* project, an expression of self-determination by a self-styled "people" to rule over a territory.

As colonialism and white domination came under fire in international circles, South Africa's government kept trying to echo the ideological framework of the rest of the world. Africans would benefit from "separate development," comparing favorably, so it was claimed, to the material possibilities of "developing" African countries. Then, South Africa asserted that the territories that had been "reserved" for Africans—a small fraction of the total farmland for a large majority of the population—constituted their genuine places of belonging and would become self-ruling in their own way. Africans would not be citizens of South Africa—not even second-class citizens—but citizens of Kwa Zulu, Bophuthatswana, or some other entity defined by a supposed ethnicity. Although the "white" economy depended on "black" labor, most Africans were considered as temporary workers (although others were granted residence rights in a complex structure of urban control manipulated by the state), who could only claim citizenship in their homeland. This tactic did not gain recognition from outside powers, and it did not end the claims of black South Africans to be equal citizens of a democratic South Africa. And while a small elite in each of the "nations" could profit from collaboration with the South African state—building patronage networks and a small state apparatus around them—black South Africans continued to demand the full rights of the South African citizen.[80]

After the colonial order collapsed around the world, maintaining racial domination in one country proved an impossible task. The government negotiated with the African National Congress for a peaceful transition to majority rule. As black South Africans flocked to the electoral bureaus for the first time in 1994, the appeal of an inclusive citizenship triumphed over the tendencies that divided citizenship had previously entailed. Citizens of South Africa have claimed social and economic as well as political rights, and the government has to a certain extent responded: supplying once-segregated, deprived urban areas with electricity and piped water, and extending pensions and welfare benefits to Africans once deprived of them, so that around 30 percent of the population is now receiving some kind of cash benefit from the state.[81] But South Africa—despite the vigorous embrace of political participation by its population and the end of legally sanctioned racial discrimination—remains one of the most unequal countries in the world. Its elite is no longer lily-white; its poorest people are almost entirely black; and controversy prevails in South African politics over both the gap between rich and poor and the corruption that grows out of patron-client relations. One response to the clash of aspirations and realizations has been to blame noncitizens, and episodes of xenophobic violence directed against Africans from neighboring countries have besmirched the triumph of a racially inclusive citizenship regime (see above).[82]

Some of the worst human consequences in Africa have followed from attempts to make state conform to nation. The failed secession attempts of Biafra from Nigeria and Katanga from the Congo in the 1960s led to years of violence. The attempt by Rwandan rulers to purify their state of its Tutsi citizens ended up in the genocide of 1994. The successful secession of Eritrea from Ethiopia produced a brutal state with little respect for the rights of citizens whose independence it claims to have won, and the successful secession of South Sudan from Sudan quickly led to a civil war between two claimants to power, each of whom mobilized ethnic divisions within the state. We see here the dangers of carrying a logic of group-based citizenship too far: there is no natural end point to the process of dividing people into categories that are supposed to represent authentic belonging and merit their own citizenship.[83]

Beyond the question of locating citizenship is the question of what citizens gain from their relationship to states. The claims made against colonial states in the decades after World War II were not just for political voice but for a better life, and the first generation of African leaders appreciated the power of such claims. But could the "nation" fulfill them any better than had the colonial state, with its larger resource base and its belated recognition that its legitimacy depended on improving the material conditions of the people whose loyalty it wanted to command? The brittleness of newly independent states had much to do with rulers' perceptions that it was extremely difficult for them to deliver their half of the citizenship bargain: decent services, decent life-chances, protection of rights in exchange for the orderly fulfillment of the citizen's obligations to the state. The world recession and the drastic decline of African economies in the late 1970s, followed by rigid programs of cutting state services imposed on cash-starved African countries by international financial institutions, destroyed much of the gains made earlier in meeting citizens' expectations.[84] In such circumstances, the temptation was strong for rulers to act in authoritarian ways and for people to try to obtain via clientage what they could not get as rights-bearing citizens.

Patrons couldn't necessarily deliver—a factor in the political convulsions in different African regimes in the 1990s. There was a certain, if halting and far from uniform, rhythm to the politics of citizenship in Africa: strong claims against colonial regimes—either to "thicken" imperial citizenship or obtain citizenship in an independent state—followed by a period of uneven efforts at forging development-oriented national states, followed by regression of both social progress and citizenship politics, and more recently a tenuous and uneven process in which some countries have experienced a revival of democratic elections, open debate, and renewed development efforts and others have experienced societal breakdown and warlordism. The mixture of vertical—patron-client—relations and horizontal—of citizens acting as such to place demands on the state—has been complex and volatile.[85]

What is left of the desires of many African political actors on the eve of independence to look beyond the territorial nation-state toward some form of federation? Three days after the collapse of the Mali Federation in August 1960, Senghor told a press conference, "Of course the federation remains an ideal. We are forced to admit that it remains a distant ideal. It cannot be realized if African states have not moved beyond their territorialism."[86] Territorialism characterized Senghor's Senegal as much as his rival's Côte d'Ivoire. Can it be overcome? The African Union, successor to the Organization of African Unity, has made modest institutional efforts to foster cooperation among states, but it has not overcome its predecessor's tendency to protect heads of state, intervening in some cases where state-based order has completely broken down but little inclined to raise questions about violations of civil, political, or human rights by member states. The clearest signs of progress are the regional associations of states, ECOWAS in West Africa and SADCC in southern Africa, limited by the same deference to heads of state, fears that such organizations could become tools of the most powerful member states, notably Nigeria and South Africa, and, in the case of peacekeeping missions, the tendency of soldiers to act as badly as those of the warlords or oppressive rulers who were the object of intervention. A small but hopeful sign: on visiting Ghana a few years ago, I saw that the direction sign at Passport Control did not distinguish foreigners from Ghanaians, but foreigners from citizens of ECOWAS countries, similar to the signs one sees on entering the European Union.

Post-Imperial Citizenship
in the European Union

The end of empire meant the separation of citizenships, but for France what ensued was both a narrowing and an expansion, narrowing in relation to Africa, expanding in relation to the rest of Europe. From 1948 to 1957, the leading French architects of European unity had argued that what should be created was in fact "Eurafrica," folding a Franco-African federation or confederation into a European confederation. To do otherwise would split France in two. African leaders took this possibility seriously, insisting that if Eurafrica came into being they should have a voice in it, just as they would have to have an equal voice as citizens of a Franco-African polity. With the final negotiations in 1957 to create the European Economic Community, it became clear that France's would-be partners did not want to take on the burdens of an ex-empire. France's African territories were relegated to the status of "associates" rather than members of the Community—with certain economic benefits but no voice. The European Economic Community would indeed be European.

In the 1990s, when the idea of a political as well as an economic European Union came back on the agenda, France joined its partners in creating a European citizenship. Citizenship in a Member State—France, Germany, Italy, etcetera— automatically conveys "citizenship of the European Union," a status to be duly imprinted on each person's passport. What European citizenship entails is a matter of controversy. With freedom of movement within the Union, citizens of one Member State have access to at least some of the social entitlements of the state in which they find themselves, and in some cases they have the right to vote in local (but not national) elections. They have the right to petition the European Parliament and to bring a legal case against their own state in European courts.[87]

Commentators have not dwelt on the fact that this citizenship strongly resembled the "superposed citizenship" that had briefly been offered to the nationals of the Member States of the French Community in 1959. France decided that it liked the idea of confederation and shared citizenship after all, but with the relatively affluent states of Europe and not with the much poorer states whose destiny had once been attached to France by colonization.

Now, years after the separation of citizenships, many people whose parents or grandparents had between 1946 and 1960 moved between African and European France with the rights of citizens are risking their lives to cross the Mediterranean to enter—without papers—a space that is European more than it is French. But the task of governing European space is not an easy one, not least where it comes to regulating legal and illicit immigration. The influx of migrants from war-torn or desperately poor parts of what used to be European empires has unleashed tensions between governments like that of Germany that favored (although more clearly in 2015 than more recently) a relatively liberal attitude toward integrating refugees into the social fabric and those like Hungary (in denial of much of its own history) that prefer to build walls.

These conflicts are part of a deeper tension between the parochialism of nation-state politics in the Member States of Europe and the vision of a coordinated European system. Europe is not a state—although it exercises an array of state-like functions—and its citizenship and its powers derive from its Member States.[88] Union institutions have a great deal to say about economic interaction, especially the free movement of capital, goods, and people. Social benefits, however, are largely a matter for each Member State to determine, although they apply—with controversies over exactly how—to both citizens of other European states and other legal residents. That poses a political problem, for the Union places fiscal constraints on each state. Especially in hard economic times—like the present—austerity is imposed on each state from what seem like distant European institutions, "dethroning politics in the name of market discipline," pushing each state "to erode social rights by necessity."[89] Told that the implacable laws of economics leave their governments no choice but to lay off civil servants or diminish benefits, many citizens in different Member States search for scapegoats—foreigners, refugees, or the European Union itself.

The strongest institutions of the Union—the European Commission, the European Central Bank, the courts—are the most removed from the controls of electoral democracy. European citizens aren't sure what the European Parliament does. Critics worry that "The technocratic basis of supranational authority is deeply at odds with the democratic presumption that citizens are competent judges of matters of public interest." Although the European citizen, even in a Member State other than his or her own, can make claims through legal action, strikes, demonstrations, and in some instances votes, such a person is regarded in some eyes as a "taxpayer" and "user" of services more than as a politically engaged person.[90]

This depoliticizing of citizenship is not unique to the European Union. When states—in the Americas, Africa, or elsewhere—outsource services to private enterprises, social benefits are distanced from the citizen's direct control. When African states rely on international NGOs to provide medical care, education, or other social services, they transfer accountability from citizens to foreign donors.[91] What is at stake in debates over how and by whom social programs are administered is the relationship between the social and the political, between the citizen as recipient and as actor in the organization of collective life.

Social Citizenship between Empire and Nation

The gains that European welfare states achieved occurred when a large portion of the people living under the jurisdiction of those states—in the colonies that is—were excluded from the benefits of social democracy. Because imperial polities like France and Britain insisted that colonized people were *inside* the polity, that they *belonged* there, that their consent and cooperation in peacetime and wartime helped make the polity strong, that there really was no other place colonized people could be, the question of what their place in the structures of imperial inclusion had to be confronted in one way or another. Although for a considerable time the distinction between the colonized subject overseas and the politically empowered citizen at home seemed to many to be natural, it kept coming under interrogation by pesky intellectuals and politicians who took their republican or democratic ideals seriously, by humanitarians of various persuasions, and most importantly by colonized people themselves who laid claim to the rights of the imperial citizen. That other activists sought to overturn colonial rule altogether raised the stakes politicians on both sides of the colonial divide had in finding the middle ground of imperial citizenship. Claim-making and political mobilization played out not just in the context of relations between colonizers and colonized, but of inter-empire rivalries that periodically underscored empires' need for the loyalty of the people they were trying to keep in a subordinate position.

When in the mid-twentieth century the states of western Europe deepened social benefits and worker protections into a basic element of citizenship, it was not so easy to segregate access to them. By the late 1940s, political and social movements in different imperial regimes were demanding the social as well as the political prerogatives of citizenship—of imperial citizenship, that is. Such demands could be and were resisted, but in the climate of uncertainty and potential conflict after the war, they were hard to ignore. The rising costs to imperial powers of social citizenship—not just the costs of administration and repression—made both colonialism as it had previously been practiced, as well as post-imperial federalism, seem like expensive alternatives to letting colonies go.

African states would have to fend their way, responding—or not—to their citizens' demands with their own resources. Before 1960, French Africans could demand as citizens that the French government provide resources for education, health, economic development, and welfare, sometimes with results. After independence, their governments could ask for foreign aid.[92] Or else, individuals could attempt to migrate, illegally or otherwise, to Europe or North America. This history of connection and disconnection—of imperial inclusion and republican exclusion—lies behind the resentments of Africans who have made it into Europe and the anxiety of Europeans in the face of people from Africa and Asia coming to their shores. What is perceived as a problem of "immigration" has deeper historical roots in the division and redivision of the world into imperial and national units.

When Senghor in 1960 warned against "territorialism"—he had previously used the word "balkanization"—among African states, he was pointing to a problem that would bedevil his own Senegal, but also the rest of the world, Europe as well as

Africa. He understood quite well that independence stood in relation to interdependence. Today, we are frequently told that we must adjust our expectations of what national states can provide to the imperatives of "globalization," but interdependence is not particularly new, and the connections involved are more specific than the term globalization suggests. The basic problem is fundamental. For a time, political leaders, intellectuals, and international relations specialists thought that a world of juridically equivalent, sovereign nation-states would be more manageable, its conflicts more defined, than the non-equivalence of political units in the age of imperialism, some of which might attempt to subordinate the others, as indeed had happened in the times of Charlemagne, Charles V, Napoleon, Hitler, and Stalin.

The violence of wars of global domination, the violence of colonial conquest, and the routinized violence of maintaining colonized people in a state of dependence and inferiority have, it seems, been consigned to the past. The banishment of colonial empire not just from the repertoires of geopolitical strategy but from the realm of the politically defensible has been the great achievement of activism in the colonial world, after decades of nonviolent mobilization as well as armed struggle. What is less clear is whether the world of juridically equivalent nation-states that has in principle replaced it can bring about the stability or the spread of social and economic progress that inspired the hopes of social and political movements. The sovereign state has become the general form of polity, but citizenship still does not have a common political, civic, or social significance. The relationship of "people," "a people," and "the people" to each other and to territory has been and remains ambiguous and contested.[93] The possibility of "civic nationalism"— where the sense of commonality flows from the project of building a democratic polity itself—has been a noble answer to a complex question, and in some parts of the world it has produced a convincing narrative. But it has never been a particularly stable one, and civic nationalism, as in post-1994 South Africa, has not proved immune from xenophobia.

It was only in the latter half of the twentieth century that citizenship in a territorially defined state came to be widely accepted as a universal norm. The point is neither to celebrate nor condemn the division of the world into national citizenships, but to understand the possibilities and limitations of the framework that has so recently emerged as the norm, in the face of both the defense of the colonial order and a range of alternative postcolonial futures. The end of colonial empires and the fiction of equivalent sovereignties have at least made it possible to *think* about global inequality, even if the forces exacerbating it now seem stronger than those inhibiting it. A half century after the collapse of colonial empires, we are left not with a sense of the triumph of aspirations for equality among states and among peoples, but with a profoundly unequal world, in which citizenship is both a powerful means for claiming resources and articulating a sense of belonging, and a concept in deep tension with the way people think of themselves and the way in which economic and political power is exercised.

The making and breaking of historical connections and both the diversity and the inequality of relationships across space leave many people uncertain of where they have a right to be, about their sense of belonging to different kinds of collectivities, about where they can exercise certain rights, about where their voices can be heard. Scholars have tried to address such issues by turning to concepts like flexible or multilevel citizenship, and at times political leaders have tried, however imperfectly, to give legal substance to such notions. Some people yearn for a citizenship that is thick in its subjective and material sustenance. Some want above all to focus the benefits of citizenship on a body they think of as a coherent whole. Many worry about the thinning out of the material benefits citizens once expected from membership in a political community. These problems are not new, and they are not about to disappear.

Citizenship in an Unequal World

MELISSA LANE CAPTURES well the conundrum of citizenship in a connected world:

> To think about citizenship is, therefore, to think about who is ideally and actually "inside" a given constitution as a citizen, who is "outside," and why. This makes it a Janus-faced ideal. It seems to articulate a universal potential, and to close it down, defining a community that is smaller than humanity and directing its members to serve each other and themselves preferentially over others.[1]

Lane is a political theorist who focuses on classical times, but her point has as much to do with the twenty-first century as the time of Aristotle. We can espouse the values attached to citizenship but take no responsibility for their violation within a state other than our own. Yet the "others" who are not being protected by their own states are now knocking on our door, challenging our humanitarian sensibilities and the closures of citizenship regimes. Such are the limits of citizenship as a normative construct.

As Léopold Sédar Senghor realized 70 years ago, there is an uneasy relationship between aspirations to independence and the actuality of interdependence. We seek to transcend this tension, but some have more means to do so than others. There are too many differences in values and interests around the world to think, beyond the most utopian imagination, of a single global citizenship enforced by a single set of institutions, and there are too many connections across borders to think of a future in enclosed blocks of citizens. The question is whether we can debate and work through these two perspectives, acknowledge particularity and commonality, and reconfigure state and international institutions that cut across such lines.[2]

Citizenship is a claim-making concept. It is therefore defined by how people act. The civil rights movement in the United States provides a good example of rights that were obtained only because people actively demanded them.[3] Citizenship is a relationship of people with each other as well as with the institutions of governance. This double relationship is why *citizenship*, as opposed to some other way of articulating affinity or another connection to a ruler, is such an important construct.[4]

Because citizenship, even in its most general and weakest form, entails membership in a political unit, the need of rulers for the loyalty or acquiescence of members enables citizens' claim-making, and hence political action and the potential for a more expansive version of citizenship. But the reverse process is also possible, and we should be wary of it. The claims of citizens to a range of social benefits for the collectivity might be thinned out, leaving citizenship as a minimum of legal protections for the self-contained individual and his or her property, eroding the very notions of social well-being and of collective action to maintain it. Arguably that is happening, in many parts of the world, before our eyes.

The units and institutions that define belonging and its benefits are themselves the object of claim-making. The history that tied citizenship to a specifically *national* form is a short one, experienced by most of the world only in the last half of the twentieth century and compromised even then by multinational federations and confederations, superposed nationalities, and group-differentiated citizenship. That rights can be articulated and defended at different levels opens the possibility of claiming them in different jurisdictions, perhaps escaping the tyranny of a majority or the conformism of a minority group.[5] That people in some historical situations successfully claim rights can encourage others to do so and foster mutual recognition of rights-bearing communities. Or claims can be narrowly focused on a putative community that seeks to prevent others from diluting its advantages. At the highest level of inclusiveness, enjoying civil, political, and social rights becomes a value that, one can argue, should apply to everyone, and such a postulate, however ambiguous and unenforceable, may be as close to global citizenship as we can get.

At the very least, economic and social rights have become discussable issues across borders. The UN, certain nongovernmental organizations, and humanitarian lobbies, as well as governments, approach issues of poverty and deprivation in the belief—widely held although not universal—that belonging to humanity should convey a chance to live a decent life. Such perceptions provide a basis for the world's poor, in whatever political context they find themselves, to make claims, and for the rich to examine their consciences. The choice is not between addressing such issues within national containers or at a global level. There is no obvious reason why the national borders of each state should contain adequate resources to produce or import sufficient water, housing, sanitation facilities, and education for its citizens. But between a focus on the claims of national citizens and an all-inclusive humanity there are many spaces and many possibilities.

Citizenship is today facing a double challenge. On the one hand, the allocation of citizens into national containers and the fiction that each is self-determining has not produced a stable pattern of international relations. Creating the semblance of such a world depended on the massive unmixing of peoples—ethnic cleansing in today's terminology—to make nation correspond to state. The violence of creating separate "Turkish" and "Greek" citizenries in the 1920s, forced population movements and self-imposed exiles after World War II, the Balkan wars of the 1990s, and the Rwandan genocide of 1994 are cases in point, and the continued turmoil in Iraq, Syria, Israel-Palestine, Turkey, Libya, and elsewhere reveal the unresolved difficulty of assigning diverse people to bounded spaces. The Islamic State repudiated the very notion of a territorial state in favor of a reimagined caliphate and a vision of people united by Islam. But Islam is not united, and the alternative the Islamic State offered is proving ephemeral, although for a time it attracted young men from countries with some of the most sophisticated versions of social citizenship in Europe. Whether the European citizenship regime can meet the challenges coming from within or the influx of refugees from without is not certain.

On the other hand, the great achievement that makes citizenship in much of the world worth defending—recognition of social rights—is under threat from the mobile forces of global capitalism. Social protections are challenged in the name of market discipline and austerity. Some commentators insist that the nation-state is the only bulwark for defending social benefits. National citizenship, with its conceit that citizens are equivalent to each other, remains part of that bulwark, but it is questionable that national units are themselves up to the task in the present conjuncture.[6] States are not mobile; people are mobile at considerable cost to themselves and their relationships; capital is the most mobile of all. The risk today is a race to the bottom, as capital moves where its social costs—notably those imposed on it by taxation and regulation—are lowest.

Advocates of market liberalization appropriate the language of citizenship for themselves, claiming that individual freedom is at stake. But such arguments entail a "redefinition of citizenship to a strictly individualistic understanding of it."[7] So far, the advocates of a transnational economic citizenship are prevailing over defenders of international norms of social citizenship. Corporations and financial institutions have developed institutional mechanisms—the World Trade Organization, arbitration panels—that enforce the "right" of capital to cross borders. Even the European Union, some argue, has proven more protective of the flow of capital and commodities than of social welfare.[8] That tendency puts pressure on states to provide less social insurance, education, environmental protection, and other benefits to citizens, and that in turn devalues the concept of citizenship itself. That retired people in Greece see their pensions devastated in the name of financial probity does not enhance faith in European, or Greek, citizenship. Xenophobic movements—blaming the increasing precarity of labor conditions on immigrants—is a response to this situation, but not a solution.[9] Citizenship is and will remain crucial to the defense of human welfare and dignity, but the question remains of whether citizenship will be narrowly focused on the individual, on his or her property, and on the bounded community of which the citizen is a "member," or whether the perceptions and institutions governing citizenship will be adaptive to the ways in which people actually move geographically and reconfigure themselves socially.

There is another side to international capital's institutional self-protection: it shows that some kinds of rights can be protected beyond the framework of national citizenship. Can we turn this situation upside down? Can we build on fledgling mechanisms that exist—international courts of justice, human rights and fair trade networks capable of publicly shaming abusive corporations—to give more substance, more "thickness," to the rights of people as they actually exist, as they move, as they lay down roots somewhere, as they remain attached to places in which they see themselves belonging? Citizenship has never meant mere affinity, but institutionalized and protected belonging. If we are to give meaning to "multilevel citizenship" or "flexible citizenship," we need to think about them in institutional terms.[10] The situation we face is not a choice between states and no states or between an all-inclusive cosmopolitanism and a narrowly bounded parochialism. The challenge is to think and act in the uneven and unequal structures in which we live.

We are not starting from zero. The Universal Declaration of Human Rights of 1948 enshrined social and economic rights, and the controversies attached to those articles at the time suggest that the issue was not window-dressing. The UN subsequently passed resolutions specifying the right of people to use and exploit their own natural resources (1952) and a Covenant on Economic, Social, and Cultural Rights (1976). The International Court of Justice and the special tribunals for Rwanda and ex-Yugoslavia have brought to justice some of the most flagrant perpetrators of crimes against humanity. There exists something on which to build. Whether transnational institutions will protect the worker in a textile factory in Bangladesh as well as a banker in Geneva is not determined by the inherent nature of those institutions; it is a political question.[11] I make no claim that such mechanisms are likely to be developed in the immediate future and would not entail problems of their own. My point is that we should not be so stuck in our categories and assumptions that we assume that the national framework is the only one available.

"Refugee" is a category in which to place the person who falls outside of a citizenship regime without disturbing the notion that each individual should be slotted into a national citizenship. Agencies like the United Nations High Commissioner for Refugees and numerous NGOs have created an institutional apparatus for helping—or channeling—refugees much more elaborate than what was available when Hannah Arendt wrote about the anomalous and dangerous position of the *apatride*. Such organizations manage camps in countries, especially in Africa and the Middle East, where the numbers of refugees vastly exceed those that have caused such consternation in Europe, and many of those families have little immediate prospect of resuming their old citizenship or assuming a new one. For them, notes Simon Turner, the ration card becomes the equivalent of the passport, and the camp managers determine the rules under which the refugees live. In effect, he writes, "The *apatride* refugee finds himself to be a citizen of the 'international community' "—but it is a peculiar kind of citizenship, not conveying political rights, not recognized outside of the refugee system.[12] As states debate how exclusionary or inclusionary they should be in regard to people with refugee status—or those who are artificially classified as "economic" rather than "political" refugees—the international order has yet to move beyond improvised solutions to a tragic situation.

Citizenship both enables and limits the possibilities people have for claiming social and economic justice within the currently constituted structure of states, and leaves those who fall outside of that structure in a perilous limbo. We have seen that from the early Roman Empire onward the commonality of citizens within a polity coexisted with social hierarchy and political oligarchy. They coexisted uneasily, for citizenship provided a framework for contestation, for some to push for greater equality and for others to use their resources to maintain and enhance their privileges. When Senghor saw politics as the conjugation of two sorts of solidarity, horizontal and vertical, he was seizing upon an oft-forgotten but essential aspect of political life. We live in a world of unequal relationships, but they are relationships nonetheless. The notion that as citizens we are all equivalent is an important mechanism for making claims; the unity of the citizenry can be a useful fiction. We belong to a political unit of some sort—or to multiple political units—and we belong to networks that may exist within or across such entities. Citizenship is a legal category; it provides a platform for insisting that a government meets certain expectations its citizens have of their state; it is built on and extends a subjective attachment to a political community. If citizenship becomes too impersonal, too legalistic, citizens may lose the sense of commonality and cooperation, but if citizens focus only on personal ties and cultural homogeneity, they entrap themselves in a closed-in world.

Sharing a common citizenship confronts us with the fact that we live with some people who are like us and some who are not. Citizenship does not in itself convey equality and it does not necessarily lead people to overcome the differences among themselves, but as in republican Rome, it provides a framework for discussion and debate about the kind of polity and society in which we wish to live. We exist as social beings, among our fellow citizens and among citizens of other polities, and we face the complexities of living in a world that is fragmented, unequal, and connected.

NOTES

Introduction. Citizenship and Belonging

1. Donald Trump, quoted in Sabrina Tavernise, "One Country, Two Tribes," *New York Times*, January 28, 2017, Review, 4.

2. Adam McKeown, *Melancholy Order: Asian Migration and the Globalization of Borders* (New York: Columbia University Press, 2008), 375.

3. Pierre Rosanvallon, *La société des égaux* (Paris: Seuil, 2011), 12, 13.

4. Over a decade ago, Seyla Benhabib concluded that the category of "national citizenship" was "no longer adequate to regulate membership." *The Rights of Others: Aliens, Residents and Citizens* (Cambridge: Cambridge University Press, 2004), 1.

5. On the need for national institutions to enforce rights deemed to be universal—but in the context of pressures from international networks and discourses—see Steve Stern and Scott Straus, "Embracing Paradox: Human Rights in the Global Age," in Stern and Straus, eds., *The Human Rights Paradox: Universality and Its Discontents* (Madison: University of Wisconsin Press, 2014), 3–28.

6. Elizabeth F. Cohen suggests that rather than see citizenship as an all-or-nothing proposition, "numerous configurations are conceivable. Because rights create political relationships it is crucial to states that they be able to disaggregate bundles of rights. The unbundling of the braid of citizenship rights has the effect of shaping and managing populations whose diverse elements could not all be governed by a single set of rules." *Semi-Citizenship in Democratic Politics* (Cambridge: Cambridge University Press, 2009), 4.

7. The intensity of these debates is emphasized in Ayelet Shachar, "Introduction: Citizenship and the 'Right to Have Rights,'" *Citizenship Studies* 18 (2014): 114–24, and the other articles in this issue. See also Leslie Holmes and Philomena Murray, eds., *Citizenship and Identity in Europe* (Aldershot: Ashgate, 1999).

8. Citizenship has been the object of thought and study for a long time. As a subject of inquiry, it received a special cachet when it got its own journal, *Citizenship Studies*, founded in 1997. The Center for the Study of Citizenship, headquartered at Wayne State University, holds an annual conference. Important compilations of studies of citizenship continue to come forth, including Ayelet Shachar, Rainer Bauböck, Irene Bloemraad, and Maarten Vink, eds., *The Oxford Handbook of Citizenship* (Oxford: Oxford University Press, 2017), a tome of 880 pages that arrived too recently to be taken into account in these pages. Routledge, however, has also published a handbook of citizenship studies that is cited below.

9. Engin Isin and Peter Nyers, "Introduction: Globalizing Citizenship Studies," in Isin and Nyers, eds., *Routledge Handbook of Global Citizenship Studies* (London: Routledge, 2014), 1–2. Kathleen Canning and Sonya Rose define citizenship as "a political status assigned to individuals by states, as a relation of belonging to specific communities, or as a set of social practices that define the relationships between peoples and states and among peoples within communities." The last clause opens the door to all sorts of relationships, which might or might not be usefully considered citizenship. Nevertheless, their relational approach has the virtue of looking beyond legal definitions toward understanding the significance of a wide range of social practices and ideas—gender prominent among them—that shape the connection of the citizen to the polity. "Gender, Citizenship and Subjectivity: Some Historical and Theoretical Considerations," *Gender and History* 13 (2001): 427–443, 427 quoted.

10. As J.G.A. Pocock writes, to think of the citizenship story as an "account of human equality excludes the greater part of the human species from access to it." "The Ideal of Citizenship Since Classical Times," in Ronald Beiner, ed., *Theorizing Citizenship* (Albany: SUNY Press, 1995), 31.

11. Benhabib (*Rights of Others*) argues against delineating lists of rights that citizenship is supposed to entail. Instead, she emphasizes that citizenship implies openness to discussion and debate over what citizenship and democracy should signify.

12. Examples of the citizen-subject controversy will be discussed later in this chapter.

13. Ralph W. Mathisen, "*Peregrini, Barbari*, and *Cives Romani*: Concepts of Citizenship and the Legal Identity of Barbarians in the Later Roman Empire," *American Historical Review* 111 (2006): 1040.

14. Frederick Cooper, *Citizenship between Empire and Nation: Remaking France and French Africa, 1945–1960* (Princeton, NJ: Princeton University Press, 2014). The British Nationality Act of 1948 also conferred a form of imperial citizenship on all inhabitants of the dominions and colonies of Great Britain, in parallel to the French law and constitution of 1946. Long before that date, many subjects of the king or queen were claiming imperial citizenship within the British Empire. Sukanya Banerjee, *Becoming Imperial Citizens: Indians in the Late-Victorian Empire* (Durham, NC: Duke University Press, 2010). Lara Putnam refers to "a vernacular theory of imperial citizenship articulated by colonials from the margins." "Citizenship from the Margins: Vernacular Theories of Rights and the State from the Interwar Caribbean," *Journal of British Studies* 53 (2014): 183.

15. Engseng Ho writes, "The coming-of-age of the new nations out of imperial tutelage in the past century can also be told as one of evictions." He is concerned with Arabs originating in the Hadramaut whose diaspora took them to many places with complex relations with many sovereigns, not just the territory that became the state of Yemen. As he describes the recent past, "Diasporas were now anomalous; everyone had to become a citizen of a state." Many were literally evicted from states—Uganda, Zanzibar, India, and others—that did not consider

Hadrami residents as their citizens. *The Graves of Tarim: Genealogy and Mobility across the Indian Ocean* (Berkeley: University of California Press, 2006), 295, 306. Even earlier, the creation of nation-states out of the Habsburg, German, and Ottoman empires in the aftermath of World War I produced an immense "unmixing of peoples." Rogers Brubaker, *Nationalism Reframed: Nationhood and the National Question in the New Europe* (Cambridge: Cambridge University Press, 1996).

16. For some of the concepts listed here, see Luis Cabrera, *The Practice of Global Citizenship* (Cambridge: Cambridge University Press, 2010); Aihwa Ong, *Flexible Citizenship: The Cultural Logics of Transnationality* (Durham, NC: Duke University Press, 1999; Willem Maas, ed., *Multilevel Citizenship* (Philadelphia: University of Pennsylvania, 2013); Will Kymlicka, *Multicultural Citizenship: A Liberal Theory of Minority Rights* (Oxford: Oxford University Press, 1995). One could add to the adjectives that have been placed before "citizenship": urban, alternative, cultural, workplace, cosmopolitan, supply-chain, therapeutic. Kristine Krause and Katharina Schramm offer this list while noting arguments for a narrower conception of citizenship as a relationship of individual and state. "Thinking Through Political Subjectivity," *African Diaspora* 4 (2011): 115–34, 125 cited.

17. Both the importance and the risks of putting multiple conceptions in play—as well as an historical record of varied and contested conceptions—are emphasized in John Clarke, Kathleen Coll, Evelina Dagnino, and Catherine Neveu, *Disputing Citizenship* (Bristol: Policy Press, 2014), esp. 10–12.

18. Holmes and Murray, *Citizenship and Identity in Europe*; Etienne Balibar, *We, the People of Europe? Reflections on Transnational Citizenship*, trans. James Swenson (Princeton, NJ: Princeton University Press, 2004); Patricia Mindus, "Dimensions of Citizenship," *German Law Journal* 15 (2014): 735–49.

19. The expression "right to have rights" comes from Hannah Arendt, *The Origins of Totalitarianism*, new ed. (New York: Harcourt Brace 1979 [1951]), 296.

20. Cohen, *Semi-Citizenship*, 47. Samuel Moyn makes a case for the 1970s as the starting point for a worldwide discourse on "human rights," but if one takes a less present-day view of what constitutes "human rights" it becomes possible to examine arguments over many years about the relationship between humanity and rights. *The Last Utopia: Human Rights in History* (Cambridge, MA: Harvard University Press, 2010).

21. Margaret Somers, *Genealogies of Citizenship: Markets, Statelessness, and the Right to Have Rights* (Cambridge: Cambridge University Press, 2008), 6–7. For other critiques of the Marshall thesis, see Michael Mann, "Ruling Class Strategies and Citizenship," and Bryan Turner, "Outline of a Theory of Citizenship," both in Bryan Turner and Peter Hamilton, eds., *Citizenship: Critical Concepts* (London: Routledge, 1994), 63–79, 199–226.

22. Nira Yuval-Davis asserts that "citizenship should not be seen as limited to state citizenship alone but should be understood as the participatory dimension

of membership in all political communities." Her focus, to be sure, is on *political community*. *The Politics of Belonging: Intersectional Contestations* (Los Angeles: Sage, 2011), 201.

23. Ong, *Flexible Citizenship*; Luicy Pedroza, "Denizen Enfranchisement and Flexible Citizenship: National Passports or Local Ballots?" in Maas, *Multilevel Citizenship*, 25–42. Citizenship questions in contemporary Africa will be discussed in chapter 3.

24. The ongoing controversy in the United States over the possible denial of admission or readmission of people from certain predominantly Muslim countries exemplifies the vulnerability of noncitizens anywhere to the vagaries of stereotyping and political gamesmanship. For another example, and not an unusual one, see Kristy Belton's discussion of children born of Haitian parents in other Caribbean countries, who lack citizenship—or at least papers—in either their place of birth or of residence. "Exclusion, Island Style: Citizenship Deprivation and Denial in the Caribbean," in Richard Marback and Marc W. Kruman, eds., *The Meaning of Citizenship* (Detroit: Wayne State University Press, 2015), 125–48.

25. Victoria Bernal, *Nation as Network: Diaspora, Cyberspace & Citizenship* (Chicago: University of Chicago Press, 2014), 12. Bernal notes that Eritreans in the diaspora provided material and moral support to their brethren during the struggle for independence from Ethiopia and a subsequent border war with Ethiopia, but more recently many of them have turned web sites that they created into an "offshore platform for civil society," something that government repression would not permit at home. Ibid., 21, 90.

26. Steven Robins, Andrea Cornwall and Bettina von Lieres, "Rethinking 'Citizenship' in the Postcolony," *Third World Quarterly* 29 (2008): 1069–86. Critiques of the citizenship concept are analyzed in Cohen, *Semi-Citizenship in Democratic Politics*, 4, and Elizabeth Jelin, "Citizenship Revisited: Solidarity, Responsibility, and Rights," in Elizabeth Jelin and Eric Hershberg, eds., *Constructing Democracy: Human Rights, Citizenship, and Society in Latin America* (Boulder: Westview, 1996), 106. A related critique focuses not on citizenship per se, but on the nation-state as an imposed container of political aspirations. Basil Davidson, *The Black Man's Burden: Africa and the Curse of the Nation-State* (New York: Times Books, 1992); Mwayila Tshiyembe, "La science politique africaniste et le statut theorique de l'État africain: Un bilan négatif," *Politique Africaine* 71 (1998): 109–32.

27. Rogers Smith, "Paths to a More Cosmopolitan Human Condition," *Daedalus* 137 (2008): 42. Krause and Schramm write, "citizenship is not everything when it comes to inclusion, voices and rights. Other forms of incorporation may coexist with (or be in conflict with) citizenship regimes." "Thinking Through Political Subjectivity," 119.

28. T. K. Oommen, *Citizenship, Nationality and Ethnicity: Reconciling Competing Identities* (Cambridge: Polity Press, 1997), 28, 234 quoted. Oommen is using "nationality" in one of two commonly employed meanings, as a sense of nationness, of being a coherent people. It is also used in a legalistic sense, as the

quality of membership in a state recognized by other states. In the legalistic meaning, citizenship refers to the rights and duties that follow from such a status. Nationality is a basis for making claims to the rights of the citizen. But neither nationality nor citizenship—and especially their relationship—have fixed meanings. They are shaped and reshaped in political processes.

29. Jürgen Habermas sees civic citizenship as "constitutional patriotism." "Citizenship and National Identity: Some Reflections on the Future of Europe," in Ronald Beiner, ed., *Theorizing Citizenship* (Albany: SUNY Press, 1995), 255–82, 264 quoted.

30. One factor behind the embrace of *jus sanguinis* by such nationally minded states as India is the desire of ruling elites to keep ties to their diasporas, a font of material resources as well as sentiment. Recognizing dual nationality, a pattern that became common in recent decades, reflects similar goals. Seyla Benhabib, "Twilight of Sovereignty or the Emergence of Cosmopolitan Norms? Rethinking Citizenship in Volatile Times," *Citizenship Studies* 11 (2007): 19–36, esp. 24.

31. For these reasons, some states in Europe that once emphasized *jus sanguinis* policies have injected *jus soli* principles. Christian Joppke and Ewa Morawska, "Integrating Immigrants in Liberal Nation-States: Policies and Practices," in Joppke and Morawska, eds., *Toward Assimilation and Citizenship: Immigrants in Liberal Nation-States* (Houndmills, UK: Palgrave Macmillan, 2003), 18.

32. Education as a mode of turning people from many milieus within the territory into a homogeneous body of citizens was in the case of France a project of the late nineteenth century. Eugen Weber, *Peasants into Frenchmen: The Modernization of Rural France, 1870–1914* (Stanford, CA: Stanford University Press, 1976).

33. Rainer Bauböck, *National Community, Citizenship and Cultural Diversity* (Vienna: Institute for Advanced Studies, 1999); Patrick Weil, *Qu'est-ce qu'un Français? Histoire de la nationalité française depuis la Révolution* (Paris: Grasset, 2002); Christian Joppke, *Immigration and the Nation-State: The United States, Germany, and Great Britain* (Oxford: Oxford University Press, 1999); Stefano Giubboni, "European Citizenship and Social Rights in Times of Crisis," *German Law Journal* 15 (2014): 935–64.

34. Gal Levy, "Contested Citizenship of the Arab Spring and Beyond," in Isin and Nyers, *Routledge Handbook of Global Citizenship Studies*, 23–37. On the enduring tension between belonging to a particular polity and more general conceptions of rights, see Bo Stråth and Quentin Skinner, "Introduction," in Quentin Skinner and Bo Stråth, eds., *States and Citizens: History, Theory, Prospects* (Cambridge: Cambridge University Press, 2003), 1–8.

35. The need for continual discussion and the balancing of conflicting imperatives is emphasized in Benhabib, *The Rights of Others*.

36. Charles Taylor "The Politics of Recognition," in Amy Gutmann, ed., *Multiculturalism* (Princeton, NJ: Princeton University Press, 1994 [1992]), 25–74; Kymlicka, *Multicultural Citizenship*, 188. One can argue that a liberal politics of

inclusion, by emphasizing the singularity of the body politic, entails a forced assimilation of minority cultures to the dominant one. See Marilyn Lake, "Citizenship as Non-Discrimination: Acceptance or Assimilationism? Political Logic and Emotional Investment in Campaigns for Aboriginal Rights in Australia, 1940 to 1970," *Gender and History* 13 (2001), 566–92.

37. On recognition, see also the work of Iris Marion Young and Nancy Fraser. Young bases her argument for group recognition on the presumption that "Social groups are comprehensive identities and ways of life." She wants to restrict such recognition to groups "which are oppressed or disadvantaged," but doesn't tell us who is to decide. "Polity and Group Difference: A Critique of Universal Citizenship," in Ronald Beiner, ed., *Theorizing Citizenship* (Albany: SUNY Press, 1995), 195; Nancy Fraser, "From Redistribution to Recognition? Dilemmas of Justice in a 'Post-Socialist' Age," *New Left Review* 212 (1995): 68–93.

38. Yuval-Davis worries that the argument for multicultural citizenship presumes "homogeneous communities with fixed boundaries which, more often as not, are defined by particular cultural agents which have been picked by the state as 'authentic' representatives." *Politics of Belonging*, 56. Similarly, Rogers Brubaker is critical of the notion of "groupism." *Ethnicity without Groups* (Cambridge, MA: Harvard University Press, 2004).

39. Rachel Giraudo and Noah Tamarkin remark, "It is not self-evident who or what 'indigenous' describes." "African Indigenous Citizenship," in Engin Insin and Peters Nyers, *Routledge Handbook of Global Citizenship Studies* (London: Routledge, 2014), 545. Bjørn Bertelsen points out that communities, defined ethnically or otherwise, are "messy," riven by competition for power within them and interacting, borrowing, and reshaping each other. "'It Will Rain Until We Are in Power!' Floods, Elections and Memory in Mozambique," in Harri Englund and Francis B. Nyamnjoh, eds., *Rights and the Politics of Recognition in Africa* (London: Zed, 2004), 171. Two pioneering texts on the construction of ethnicity in Africa are Leroy Vail, ed., *The Creation of Tribalism in Southern Africa* (Berkeley: University of California Press, 1989) and Jean-Loup Amselle and Elikia M'Bokolo, eds., *Au coeur de l'ethnie: Ethnies,tribalisme et État en Afrique* (Paris: La Découverte, 1985).

40. Kymlicka, *Multicultural Citizenship*, 101. As Saskia Sassen points out, Kymlicka and others making similar arguments look only at groups *within* nation-states and so "continue to use the nation-state as the normative frame and to understand the social groups involved as parts of national civil society." "Toward Post-National and Denationalized Citizenship," in Engin Isin and Bryan Turner, eds., *Handbook of Citizenship Studies* (Thousand Oaks, CA: Sage 2002), 281. Yuval-Davis (*Politics of Belonging*, 65) also warns of the danger of naturalizing the nation-state at the same time as reifying minority cultures.

41. Lucien Jaume, "Citizen and State under the French Revolution," in Skinner and Stråth, *States and Citizens*, 131–44. As Dominique Colas points out, the idea of an "indivisible" republic that dates to the French Revolution counters not so much spatial or territorial divisions as "social groups." *Citoyenneté et nationalité* (Paris: Gallimard, 2004), 60.

42. Atul Kohli, "India: Federalism and the Accommodation of Ethnic Nationalism," in Ugo M. Amoretti and Nancy Bermeo, eds., *Federalism and Territorial Cleavages* (Baltimore: Johns Hopkins University Press, 2004), 281–99.

43. "Haryana State in India Proposes New Caste Status in Bid to Quell Protests," *New York Times*, February 22, 2016. Sudipta Kaviraj argues that "Most major radical demands in Indian politics are now for group equality rather than income equality between individuals." "A State of Contradictions: The Post-colonial State in India," in Skinner and Stråth, *States and Citizens*, 145–63, 160 quoted.

44. The insistence on a singular civic culture rooted in the French Revolution, which one still sees even in progressive circles, reminds me of a remark of an opponent of extending citizenship to people in the colonies in 1946: to be French, his argument went, meant "to participate in the blood, the spirit, the soul of Joan of Arc, Sully, Richelieu, Louis XIV, Colbert, Napoleon, Clemenceau." A rather tall order for a colonial subject or an immigrant. "Projet d'une Constitution de l'Empire Français," annex to transcript of meeting of 14 November 1944 of Conseil Consultative de l'Empire Français, 100APOM/898, Archives d'Outre-Mer, Aix-en-Provence. As distinguished a political scientist as Dominique Schnapper presents a vision of the historical roots of the citizenry of the nation that—while it doesn't go back to Joan of Arc—defines a singularity of community that many people in today's France would find hard to identify with. *La Communauté des citoyens: Sur l'idée moderne de nation* (Paris: Gallimard, 1994). In seeing this history as the basis of the community of citizens, she not only affirms her opposition to an ethnic conception of "Frenchness" but denies the relevance of any other sort of attachment that people might bring with them to France: "It is the effort of tearing away identities and affinities that are lived as natural by the abstraction of citizenship that characterizes in itself the national project. *There exists only one idea of the nation*." Ibid., 24 (emphasis in original).

45. An extensive literature on immigration and citizenship in France includes Clifford Rosenberg, *Policing Paris: The Origins of Modern Immigration Control between the Wars* (Ithaca, NY: Cornell University Press, 2006) and Mary Dewhurst Lewis, *The Boundaries of the Republic: Migrant Rights and the Limits of Universalism in France, 1918–1940* (Stanford, CA: Stanford University Press, 2007). Local communities in past and present, not just states, have worried about the influx of the poor and the rootless. See Beate Althammer, Lutz Raphael, and Tamara Stazic-Wendt, eds., *Rescuing the Vulnerable: Poverty, Welfare and Social Ties in Modern Europe* (New York: Berghahn Books, 2016).

46. Yuval-Davis, *Politics of Belonging*, 57; Leslie Holmes and Philomena Murray, "Introduction," in Holmes and Murray, eds., *Citizenship and Identity in Europe* (Aldershot: Ashgate, 1999), 2.

47. Yuval-Davis (*Politics of Belonging*, 47) writes, "the notion of 'the citizen', unlike that of 'the subject', is usually marked by at least a certain sense of entitlement, an important public emotion which is crucial in various political projects of belonging."

48. Rogers Smith points out that citizenship has rarely been unitary, but that "the struggle against second-class citizenship" in the United States has focused

on claims for "unitary or uniform citizenship," in which each individual had "exactly the same bundle of rights and duties, especially voting rights, property rights, and due process rights." Some of the most important social movements in American history have insisted that "Separate could not be equal citizenship, for the races, for the genders, for any subgroup of citizens." "The Questions Facing Citizenship in the Twenty-First Century," in Richard Marback and Marc Kruman, eds., *The Meaning of Citizenship* (Detroit: Wayne State University Press, 2015), 14; Isin and Nyers, "Introduction," in Isin and Nyers, *Routledge Handbook of Global Citizenship Studies*, 8.

49. On women citizens as both subjects and objects of politics in India, see Mrinalini Sinha, *Specters of Mother India: The Global Restructuring of an Empire* (Durham, NC: Duke University Press, 2006).

50. Willem Maas, "Varieties of Multilevel Citizenship," in Maas, *Multilevel Citizenship*, 2.

51. The category of "dhimmi" marked the place—recognized but not equal—of non-Muslim communities within an Islamic polity.

52. Gianluca Parolin, *Citizenship in the Arab World: Kin, Religion and Nation-State* (Amsterdam: Amsterdam University Press, 2009); Michelle Campos, *Ottoman Brothers: Muslims, Christians, and Jews in Early Twentieth-Century Palestine* (Stanford, CA: Stanford University Press, 2010).

53. Benhabib, *The Rights of Others*; Smith, "Paths to a More Cosmopolitan Human Condition." The Universal Declaration of 1948 provided a starting point, and subsequent conventions and the creation of international courts, however limited their purview, provide a framework for extending the notion of rights to a global level.

54. Yasemin Nuhoğlu Soysal, *Limits of Citizenship: Migrants and Postnational Membership in Europe* (Chicago: University of Chicago Press, 1994). Sassen, "Towards Post-National and Denationalized Citizenship,"277–91, distinguishes forms of citizenship that modify current forms of national citizenship from those that posit alternative conceptions. Both she and Soysal see these developments as a reflection of increased mobility and communication of recent decades and do not explore the much older roots of citizenship beyond nation-states. For a critique of the concept of post-national citizenship, see Joppke, *Immigration and the Nation-State*, 141–46, 268–71.

55. Niraja Gopal Jayal, "Indian Citizenship: A Century of Disagreement," in Isin and Nyers, *Routledge Handbook of Global Citizenship Studies*, 401.

56. As Rosanvallon puts it, in the act of voting the individual "finds himself stripped of his determinations and belongings." This abstraction is the "basis of the development of the idea of political equality." *Société des égaux*, 57. But he notes that at first French citizens voted in assemblies in each canton, and it was only in 1913 that the secret ballot (*isoloir*) was introduced; up to then the vote itself, not just queuing to vote, was a social act. Ibid., 59–60.

57. On the Russian model, see Jane Burbank, "An Imperial Rights Regime: Law and Citizenship in the Russian Empire," *Kritika* 7 (2006): 397–431.

58. Silyane Larcher, *L'autre citoyen: L'idéal républicain et les Antilles après l'esclavage* (Paris: Colin, 2014); Uday Singh Mehta, *Liberalism and Empire: A Study in Nineteenth Century British Liberal Thought* (Chicago: University of Chicago Press, 1999).

59. Rogers Brubaker, *Citizenship and Nationhood in France and Germany* (Cambridge, MA: Harvard University Press, 1992). For a critique and alternative concepts from the French side, see Weil, *Qu'est-ce qu'un Français?* On the German side see Geoff Eley and Jan Palmowski, eds., *Citizenship and National Identity in Twentieth-Century Germany* (Stanford, CA: Stanford University Press, 2008) and Eli Nathans, *The Politics of Citizenship in Germany: Ethnicity, Utility and Nationalism* (Oxford: Berg, 2004).

60. Engin Isin and Bryan Turner, "Citizenship Studies: An Introduction," in Isin and Turner, eds., *Handbook of Citizenship Studies* (Beverly Hills: Sage, 2002), 2, 8; Bauböck, *National Community*, 5–6; Frances Hagopian, "Latin American Citizenship and Democratic Theory," in Joseph Tulchin and Meg Ruthenburg, eds., *Citizenship in Latin America* (Boulder, CO: Lynne Rienner, 2007), 14. The thin-thick distinction is more useful than one from the political philosopher James Tully that has received a certain amount of attention: between "modern" and "diverse" citizenship. As should be clear by now, "modern"—in the chronological sense—conceptions of citizenship are quite diverse. And while it is worthwhile to draw attention to the many ways in which people conceptualize belonging and political community that are distinct from "modern" states' emphasis on legal categories (Tully's main point), aggregating them as "diverse" is a contemporary scholar's conceit, since taken individually, each form of citizenship might be as monolithic as the one Tully is criticizing. *On Global Citizenship: James Tully in Dialogue* (London: Bloomsbury, 2014).

61. Sassen refers to a "thinning" of social citizenship in Marshall's sense of the term. "Towards Post-National and Denationalized Citizenship," 280. Bryan Turner sees the distinction between a "denizen"—a legal resident without citizenship rights—and a citizen being diminished as social benefits are reduced. "We Are All Denizens Now: On the Erosion of Citizenship," *Citizenship Studies* 20 (2016): 679–92.

62. Schnapper, *Communauté des citoyens,* 197–98; Stéphane Caporal, "L'Europe et le Citoyen," in Association Française des Historiens des Idées Politiques, *Sujet et Citoyen: Actes du Colloque de Lyon (11–12 septembre 2003)* (Aix-en-Provence: Presses Universitaires d'Aix-Marseille, 2004), 450.

63. Yuval-Davis (*Politics of Belonging*, 54) emphasizes that the idea of citizenship in a nation-state presumes "a closed society in a reality which does not fully correspond to this."

64. Clarke et al., *Disputing Citizenship*, 11–12. Balibar stresses "the continued creation of citizenship (*dēmos*) through collective action and the acquisition of fundamental rights to existence, work, and expression, as well as civic equality and the equal dignity of languages, classes, and sexes." *We, the People of Europe*, 9.

Chapter 1. Imperial Citizenship from the Roman Republic to the Edict of Caracalla

1. Emma Dench warns against mythmaking in the backward projections onto Roman citizenship of today's concerns with multicultural or cosmopolitan societies, rejection of racism, and open societies. She points out that the Roman example has been used as a model for fascism as well as for multicultural citizenship. *Romulus' Asylum: Roman Identities from the Age of Alexander to the Age of Hadrian* (Oxford: Oxford University Press, 2005), 20, 25, 95–96.

2. The reference is to Diogenes. A. A. Long, "The Concept of the Cosmopolitan in Greek and Roman Thoughts," *Daedalus* 137 (2008): 50–58, esp. 50; Ralph W. Mathisen, "*Peregrini, Barbari*, and *Cives Romani*: Concepts of Citizenship and the Legal Identity of Barbarians in the Later Roman Empire," *American Historical Review* 111 (2006): 1012. More generally, see the chapter "Citizenship" in Melissa Lane, *The Birth of Politics: Eight Greek and Roman Political Ideas and Why They Matter* (Princeton, NJ: Princeton University Press, 2014). Derek Heater argues that the idea of world citizen, looking beyond the state, was transmitted from Greece to Rome, was then taken up by scholars in the Renaissance and Enlightenment, and resurfaced in certain quarters after 1945. *World Citizenship and Government: Cosmopolitan Ideas in the History of Western Political Thought* (Houndsmill, UK: Macmillan, 1996), 170–76.

3. Lane, 291, citing Aelius Aristides in AD 155. Tacitus asserted that Rome enfranchised people they conquered whereas Athens treated them as foreigners. Romans made much of their apparent openness; the story of Aeneas can be read as a myth underscoring the immigrant origins of the Roman elite. Dench, however, warns against exaggerating the differences with Athens: "Mobility, and elite mobility in particular, was a normal state of affairs in the archaic Mediterranean world as families exercised social and economic networks in a world within which ethnic and state boundaries were still fluid." *Romulus' Asylum*, 98, 102–4, 121–22, 121 quoted.

4. Claude Nicolet, *The World of the Citizen in Republican Rome*, trans. P. S. Falla (London: Batsford, 1980 [1976]), 22–23.

5. Clifford Ando, *Roman Social Imaginaries: Language and Thought in Contexts of Empire* (Toronto: University of Toronto Press, 2015), 12, 23.

6. Nigel Pollard, "The Roman Army," in David Potter, ed., *A Companion to the Roman Empire* (Oxford: Blackwell, 2006), 211, 222–23.

7. Dench, *Romulus' Asylum*, 124.

8. Jean-Michel David, "Rome: Citoyenneté et espace politique," in Claude Fiévet, ed., *Invention et réinvention de la citoyenneté* (Pau: Editions Joëlle Sampy, 2000), 81–93, 89 quoted; Mathisen, "*Peregrini*," 1016.

9. J.G.A. Pocock looks at Roman citizenship through the eyes of the jurist Gaius, who focused on the relationship of persons, actions, and things—not just relations among persons or political ideals (the more Aristotelian approach). A person's control of and access to things was regulated under law. The person became the citizen, Pocock writes, "through the possession of things and the

practice of jurisprudence." "The Ideal of Citizenship Since Classical Times," in Ronald Beiner, ed., *Theorizing Citizenship* (Albany: SUNY Press, 1995), 34–35.

10. Another category was that of the freed slave, freed that is by the decision of his or her owner. Since the act of manumission was considered a fictive filial bond, slaves who were freed were in effect reborn and acquired the civic status of the master, although they would be excluded from political and military roles by virtue of their lack of resources. The emperor Augustus apparently feared that the category of citizen was being diluted, and perhaps endangered, by the entry of too many freemen into it, and he put in place restrictions on manumission, but it is unclear how much of an impact these measures had. Henrik Mouritsen, *The Freedman in the Roman World* (Cambridge: Cambridge University Press, 2011),70, 79–90.

11. Jonathan Edmondson, "Cities and Urban Life in the Western Provinces of the Roman Empire, 30 BCE–250 CE," in David Potter, ed., *A Companion to the Roman Empire* (Oxford: Blackwell, 2006), 255–58, 273–74, 274 quoted.

12. Nicolet, *World of the Citizen*, 215 quoted, 311, 320.

13. Mary Beard, *SPQR: A History of Ancient Rome* (New York: Liveright/ Norton, 2015), 237–40; Nicolet, *World of the Citizen*, 23.

14. Nicolet, *World of the Citizen*, 44.

15. Greg Woolf, *Becoming Roman: The Origins of Provincial Civilization in Gaul* (Cambridge: Cambridge University Press, 1998), 39–40.

16. Nicolet, *World of the Citizen*, 317.

17. Clifford Ando, "The Administration of the Provinces," in Potter, 187.

18. Peter Garnsey, "Roman Citizenship and Roman Law in the Late Empire," in Simon Swain and Mark Edwards, eds., *Approaching Late Antiquity: The Transformation from Early to Late Empire*, Oxford Scholarship on Line (*www.oxfordscholarship.com*), 2010 [2006], 5. On the place of colonies in relation to Roman citizenship, see A. N. Sherwin-White, *The Roman Citizenship* (Oxford: Clarendon Press, 1973), 76–94. He notes the distinction between a "Latin colony"—an incorporative institution to bring in Latins—and a "citizen colony"—an outpost of Roman citizenship. The former, he asserts, were "supplementary" to the latter (77).

19. Joy Connolly, *The Life of Roman Republicanism* (Princeton, NJ: Princeton University Press, 2015), 13.

20. Ibid., 19.

21. Ibid., 32, 47, 52, 55. Dench (*Romulus' Asylum*, 111) glosses Cicero as arguing that citizenship was an ideal "from which contemporary Rome has fallen short."

22. Connolly, *The Life of Roman Republicanism*, 76, 93.

23. Ibid., 155.

24. Pocock suggests that "the growth of jurisprudence decentres and may marginalize the assembly of citizens by the enormous diversity of answers it brings to the questions of where and by whom law is made." "Ideal of Citizenship," 39–40.

25. Nicolet, *World of the Citizen*, 21; Pocock, "The Ideal of Citizenship," 38–39. Dench (*Romulus' Asylum*, 133) suggests that Caesar's granting of citizenship

to many people in Gaul was a sign of incipient monarchy—lining up supporters for the leader.

26. Greg Rowe, "The Emergence of Monarchy: 44 BCE–96 CE," in David Potter, ed., *A Companion to the Roman Empire* (Oxford: Blackwell, 2006), 114; Connolly, 200.

27. Rowe, 120, 123.

28. Clifford Ando, "The Administration of the Provinces," in David Potter, ed., *A Companion to the Roman Empire* (Oxford: Blackwell, 2006), 182, 189–90; Maud W. Gleason, "Greek Cities under Roman Rule," in ibid., 228–29.

29. Paul Fontaine, "De Lyon à Rome—Africains et Syriens en Europe de l'Ouest sous l'Empire romain," paper presented to conference on "Empire, Labour, Citizenship," Vrije Universiteit Brussel, November 18, 2015; Beard, *SPQR*, 521.

30. Clifford Ando, "Sovereignty, Territoriality, and Universalism in the Aftermath of Caracalla," in Clifford Ando, ed., *Citizenship and Empire in Europe 200–1900: The Antonine Constitution after 1800 Years* (Stuttgart: Franz Steiner Verlag, 2016), 7–28.

31. Garnsey, "Roman Citizenship and Roman Law," 2–3; Myles Lavan, "The Spread of Roman Citizenship, 14–212 CE: Quantification in the Face of High Uncertainty," *Past and Present* 230 (2016): 3–46. On rapid implementation of the edict in Asia Minor, see Georgy Kantor, "Local Law in Asia Minor after the *Constitutio Antoniniana*," in Clifford Ando, ed., *Citizenship and Empire in Europe 200–1900: The Antonine Constitution after 1800 Years* (Stuttgart: Franz Steiner Verlag, 2016), 49–52.

32. Beard, *SPQR*, 527. Beard adds, "After a thousand years, Rome's 'citizenship project' had been completed and a new era had begun. It was not an era of peaceful, multicultural equality, though." Ibid., 529.

33. Mathisen, *"Peregrini,"* 1015.

34. Ibid., 1016, 1019–25, 1035.

35. Garnsey, "Roman Citizenship and Roman Law," 7–8, Nicolet, *World of the Citizen*, 47. Mathisen, *"Peregrini,"* 1017, claims that with the Christianization of the Roman Empire, full citizenship came to be based on Christian status, narrowing the concept in relation to the empire but giving rise to the metaphorical notion of citizenship in a broader community, the "city of God."

36. Lane sees that the tension in classical times between the principle of citizens' voice in politics and the practical limits of their control exhibits an "uncomfortable closeness to predicaments of our own." *Birth of Politics*, 290.

Chapter 2. Citizenship and Empire—Europe and Beyond

1. As Ralph Mathisen writes, "As the Roman afterglow petered out, Roman concepts of citizenship, whether of a world, a nation, a province, or a city, did likewise, to be replaced in the Middle Ages by models of subjugation to bishops and kings." *"Peregrini, Barbari,* and *Cives Romani*: Concepts of Citizenship

and the Legal Identity of Barbarians in the Later Roman Empire," *American Historical Review* 111 (2006): 1039. Cities were the biggest exception to this generalization.

2. The other German formula used is *Staatangehörigkeit*, whose root is in the word for belonging and is often translated as nationality, minus the urban connotation.

3. Max Weber, "Citizenship in Ancient and Medieval Cities," in Gershon Shafir, ed., *The Citizenship Debates: A Reader* (Minneapolis: University of Minnesota Press, 1998), 43–49.

4. Neither "Spain" nor "Portugal" was a "predefined entity" before, during, and after the period in the sixteenth and seventeenth centuries when a single monarch presided over both kingdoms. Many people hesitated between loyalty to the unified monarchy and desire for a distinctly Portuguese kingdom. Tamar Herzog's arguments are developed in *Defining Nations: Immigrants and Citizens in Early Modern Spain and Spanish America* (New Haven: Yale University Press, 2003); "Communities Becoming a Nation: Spain and Spanish America in the Wake of Modernity (and Thereafter)," *Citizenship Studies* 11 (2007): 151–72; and *Frontiers of Possession: Spain and Portugal in Europe and the Americas* (Cambridge, MA: Harvard University Press, 2015), 252 quoted.

5. At first, some argued that only Castilians had the right to settle or trade with the Americas, but the people of Aragon and then Navarre pressed, with some success, to be included. Herzog, *Frontiers of Possession*, 56–60.

6. Tamar Herzog, "The Appropriation of Native Status: Forming and Reforming Insiders and Outsiders in the Spanish Colonial World," *Rechtsgeschichte/ Legal History* 22 (2014): 140–49, esp. 143.

7. On the relationship between natural law and citizens' rights in early-modern European empires, see Annabel S. Brett, "The Development of the Idea of Citizens' Rights," in Quentin Skinner and Bo Stråth, eds., *States and Citizens: History, Theory, Prospects* (Cambridge: Cambridge University Press, 2003), 97–114.

8. Herzog, *Frontiers of Possession*, 116–27; Herzog, "Communities," 157–59.

9. Matthew C. Mirow, *Latin American Constitutions: The Constitution of Cádiz and Its Legacy in Spanish America* (Cambridge. Cambridge University Press, 2015), 2, 4.

10. Jeremy Adelman points out that merchants "stopped short of a full-blown critique" of the empire's mercantilist system of trade. In terms of politics, "They did not want a new regime so much as a restored old one." *Sovereignty and Revolution in the Iberian Atlantic* (Princeton, NJ: Princeton University Press, 2006), 140, 144.

11. Mirow, *Latin American Constitutions*, 38, 77. Mirow claims that the American deputies asserted both equality with the Peninsular Spanish and the distinctiveness of their experience. Ibid, 78, 90. Brian Hamnett points out that constitutional alternatives were set forth in some Spanish American territories between 1811 and 1816 independent of the Cádiz process. *The End of Iberian*

Rule on the American Continent, 1770–1830 (Cambridge: Cambridge University Press, 2017), 176–77.

12. Adelman, *Sovereignty and Revolution*; Benedict Anderson, *Imagined Communities: Reflections on the Origin and Spread of Nationalism* (London: Verso, 1983). Adelman situates the Spanish case in a broader context of the late eighteenth and early nineteenth centuries, emphasizing struggles within and among empires rather than a general trajectory from empire to nation-state. "An Age of Imperial Revolutions," *American Historical Review* 113 (2008): 319–40.

13. Some in the Cortes argued, unsuccessfully, for giving constitutional recognition to multiple communities or nations within the empire. Herzog, "Communities becoming a Nation," 156–57; Hamnett, *End of Iberian Rule*, 182.

14. Josep M. Fradera, "Tainted Citizenship and Imperial Constitutions: The Case of the Spanish Constitution of 1812," in Clifford Ando, ed., *Citizenship and Empire in Europe 200–1900: The Antonine Constitution after 1800 Years* (Stuttgart: Franz Steiner Verlag, 2016), 223, 232; Herzog, "Communities," 157; Hamnett, *End of Iberian Rule*, 194–95; Marixa Lasso, "A Republican Myth of Racial Harmony: Race and Patriotism in Colombia, 1810–12," *Historical Reflections/ Réflexions Historiques* 29 (2003): 43–63. After the loss of the mainland American colonies, Spain continued to use the notion of "special" laws for what remained, an increasingly sharp point of conflict with the citizens of the Spanish islands. Josep M. Fradera, "L'esclavage et la logique constitutionnelle des empires," *Annales: Histoire, Sciences Sociales* 63 (2008): 533–62, esp. 537–40, 548–49. See also Christopher Schmidt-Nowara, *The Conquest of History: Spanish Colonialism and National Histories in the Nineteenth Century* (Pittsburgh: University of Pittsburgh Press, 2006).

15. Herzog, "Communities," 157–60. Mirow (*Latin American Constitutions*, 63) sees the distinction between "Spaniards"—a category inclusive of the peoples of American territory controlled by Spain—and "citizens"—who possessed political as well as civil rights—as stemming from the French model that separated active and passive citizens. Women, like people of African descent and servants, were regarded as lacking the autonomy necessary to make political decisions.

16. Adelman, *Sovereignty and Revolution*, esp. 188–89, 194–96; Hamnett, *End of Iberian Rule*, 183. On the often intense debates over numbers and criteria for representations, see Mirow, *Latin American Constitutions*, 91–99. Some argued that Indians were not culturally qualified to vote, others insisted that they were integral parts of the political community, drawing on arguments about preconquest civilizations, the writings of las Casas, and doctrines of Catholic monarchy emphasizing the King's authority over Indian subjects. Ibid., 92. The issue of overseas citizens possibly outnumbering those of the metropole would surface in the debates over the French Constitution of 1946, in a warning that France might become "the colony of its former colonies." That debate is discussed briefly in chapter 3 and at length in Frederick Cooper, *Citizenship between Empire and Nation: Remaking France and French Africa, 1945–1960* (Princeton, NJ: Princeton University Press, 2014).

17. Fradera, "Tainted Citizenship and Imperial Constitutions," 226; Josep M. Fradera, "Empires in Retreat: Spain and Portugal after the Napoleonic Wars," in Alfred McCoy, Josep Fradera, and Stephen Jacobson, eds., *Endless Empire: Spain's Retreat, Europe's Eclipse, America's Decline* (Madison: University of Wisconsin Press, 2012), 59–61.

18. Mirow, *Latin American Constitutions*, 31, 41–42, 48, 58, 61, 93. The Cortes made some attempts to recognize the rights of certain Indian communities to land, but the process soon ran into vested interests. Ibid., 93.

19. Hamnett, *End of Iberian Rule*, 4.

20. Adelman, *Sovereignty and Revolution*, 264, 366.

21. Anderson, *Imagined Communities*, 16; Adelman, esp. 271, 277–81, 360–67. The Cádiz constitution was reinstated in Spain and parts of the Americas still controlled by Spain in 1820. Mirow, 113.

22. Rebecca Scott, *Slave Emancipation in Cuba: The Transition to Free Labor, 1860–1899* (Princeton, NJ: Princeton University Press, 1985); Rebecca Scott, *Degrees of Freedom: Louisiana and Cuba after Slavery* (Cambridge, MA: Harvard University Press, 2005); Ada Ferrer, *Insurgent Cuba: Race, Nation, and Revolution, 1868–1898* (Chapel Hill: University of North Carolina Press, 1999); and Christopher Schmidt-Nowara, *Empire and Antislavery: Spain, Cuba, and Puerto Rico, 1833–1874* (Pittsburgh: University of Pittsburgh Press, 1999).

23. Adelman, *Sovereignty and Revolution*, 396. The new constitutions usually excluded people from Iberian Spain from the new citizenries, consistent with the revolutionary separation from Spain. But many Spaniards had their place in local communities in the Americas and the lines were not so easy to draw. The old tradition of defining "belonging" by specific social relations with specific communities continued. Herzog, "Communities," 162.

24. Mirow, *Latin American Constitutions*, 66, 141–43.

25. Marcela Echeverri, "Race, Citizenship, and the Cádiz Constitution in Popayán (New Granada)," in Natalia Sobrevilla Perea and Scott Eastman, eds., *The Rise of Constitutional Government in the Iberian Atlantic World: The Impact of the Cádiz Constitution of 1812* (Tuscaloosa: University of Alabama Press, 2015), 91–110; The Portuguese constitution of 1820 was more inclusive of the free colored population, but other actions limited their voting rights. Fradera, "Empires in Retreat," 62–63.

26. James Sanders, *Contentious Republicans: Popular Politics, Race, and Class in Nineteenth-Century Colombia* (Durham, NC: Duke University Press, 2004), 193. Sanders sees the openings that "subalterns" were able to forge closing down later in the century, especially in the 1880s. See also Aline Helg, *Liberty and Equality in Caribbean Colombia, 1770–1835* (Chapel Hill: University of North Carolina Press, 2004), and Jason McGraw, *The Work of Recognition: Caribbean Colombia and the Postemancipation Struggle for Citizenship* (Chapel Hill: University of North Carolina Press, 2014). McGraw argues that Colombian slaves wanted not only freedom but recognition as a collectivity that had gone through a particular experience, and that they sought to articulate a "vernacular

citizenship" in many aspects of daily life. Formalized equality combined with extreme inequality in access to property and conceptions of cultural hierarchy made for long-term struggles over inclusion and exclusion in a Colombian nation.

27. Hilda Sabato, "Review Essay: On Political Citizenship in Nineteenth-Century Latin America," *American Historical Review* 106 (2001): 1290–1315, esp. 1295, 1297, 1301. See also her "Citizenship, Political Participation and the Formation of the Public Sphere in Buenos Aires 1850s–1880s," *Past and Present* 136 (1992): 139–63. As Mirow notes (*Latin American Constitutions*, 124), indigenous communities gained citizenship and the vote alongside everybody else, but lost the use of institutions (Indian councils and *caciques*) that had afforded them a certain kind of representation.

28. Clément Thibaud, "Race et citoyenneté dans les Amériques (1770–1910), *Le Mouvement Social* 252 (2015): 5–19, 14 quoted.

29. Frances Hagopian, "Latin American Citizenship and Democratic Theory," in Joseph Tulchin and Meg Ruthenburg, eds., *Citizenship in Latin America* (Boulder, CO: Lynne Rienner, 2007), 21, 36–37. See also James Holston, "Citizenship in Disjunctive Democracies," in Tulchin and Ruthenburg, *Citizenship in Latin America*, 75–94.

30. Evalina Dagnino, "Citizenship in Latin America: An Introduction," *Latin American Perspectives* 30, 2 (2003): 5.

31. James Holston, *Insurgent Citizenship: Disjunctions of Democracy and Modernity in Brazil* (Princeton, NJ: Princeton University Press, 2008), 7 quoted.

32. Hagopian, "Latin American Citizenship and Democratic Theory," 43–44.

33. Dagnino, "Citizenship in Latin America," 216.

34. David Armitage, *The Ideological Origins of the British Empire* (Cambridge: Cambridge University Press, 2000); Eliga Gould, *The Persistence of Empire: British Political Culture in the Age of the American Revolution* (Chapel Hill: University of North Carolina Press, 2000).

35. Michelle Everson suggests that the lack of clarity of what constituted Britishness and where exactly the British state was located was both problematic and potentially useful to claims for inclusion. Instead of specifying an indivisible sovereignty on a clearly defined body of people, British law left space for "a far more complex scheme of fragmented and interlocking sovereignties with far smaller, self-defining communities forming the basis for true community, and thus for sustainable substantive equality." "'Subjects,' or 'Citizens of Erewhon'? Law and Non-Law in the Development of a 'British Citizenship,'" *Citizenship Studies* 7 (2003), 57–84, 83 quoted.

36. The quoted phrase is from a British law journal from 1902, cited in Rieko Karatani, *British Citizenship: Empire, Commonwealth and Modern Britain* (London: Cass, 2003), 3–4. Karatani (3) emphasizes the "fuzzy," "vague," and "malleable" nature of Britishness and the ambiguous relationship of such notions to legal status.

37. Margaret Somers, "Rights, Relationality, and Membership: Rethinking the Making and Meaning of Citizenship," *Law and Social Inquiry* 19 (1994): 63–112.

38. Christopher Brown, *Moral Capital: Foundations of British Abolitionism* (Chapel Hill: University of North Carolina Press, 2006); Seymour Drescher, *Abolition: A History of Slavery and Antislavery* (Cambridge: Cambridge University Press, 2009).

39. P. J. Marshall, *The Making and Unmaking of Empires: Britain, India, and America, c. 1750–1783* (New York: Oxford University Press, 2005).

40. Gould, *The Persistence of Empire*. On indigenous peoples'—including Native Americans'—use of imperial law, courts, and other institutions, see Saliha Belmessous, ed., *Native Claims: Indigenous Law against Empire, 1500–1920* (Oxford: Oxford University Press, 2011). On the complexity of settler power and legal jurisdiction, see Lisa Ford, *Settler Sovereignty: Jurisdiction and Indigenous People in America and Australia, 1788–1836* (Cambridge, MA: Harvard University Press, 2010).

41. David C. Hendrickson, *Peace Pact: The Lost World of the American Founding* (Lawrence: University Press of Kansas, 2003).

42. Gary Lawson and Guy Seidman, *The Constitution of Empire: Territorial Expansion and American Legal History* (New Haven: Yale University Press, 2004).

43. Douglas Bradburn, " 'True Americans' and 'Hordes of Foreigners': Nationalism, Ethnicity and the Problem of Citizenship in the United States, 1789–1800," *Historical Reflections/Réflexions Historiques* 29 (2003): 19–41, esp. 21–22.

44. Adam McKeown, *Melancholy Order: Asian Migration and the Globalization of Borders* (New York: Columbia University Press, 2008).

45. Thomas Alexander Aleinikoff, *Semblances of Sovereignty: The Constitution, the State, and American Citizenship* (Cambridge, MA: Harvard University Press, 2002).

46. In discussing citizenship over the sweep of US history, Judith Shklar emphasizes the "exclusions and inclusions, in which xenophobia, racism, religious bigotry, and fear of alien conspiracies have played their part," but she emphasizes above all the problem of slavery. She makes clear that citizenship concepts were not static but were rooted in social and political contexts and in political struggle. *American Citizenship: The Quest for Inclusion* (Cambridge, MA: Harvard University Press, 1991), 4 quoted, 13, 15.

47. Duncan Bell, *The Idea of Greater Britain: Empire and the Future of World Order, 1860–1900* (Princeton, NJ: Princeton University Press, 2007); Daniel Gorman, *Imperial Citizenship: Empire and the Question of Belonging* (Manchester: Manchester University Press, 2006). New Zealanders and others sometimes referred to themselves as "neo-Britains," claiming two kinds of belonging at the same time. J.G.A. Pocock, *The Discovery of Islands: Essays in British History* (Cambridge: Cambridge University Press, 2005), 187.

48. Thomas Holt, *The Problem of Freedom: Race, Labor, and Politics in Jamaica and Britain, 1832–1938* (Baltimore: Johns Hopkins University Press, 1992).

49. Fradera ("L'esclavage et logique constitutionnelle," 550–60) makes this contrast. He notes as well that the rebellion of 1865 occurred only a few years after the "Mutiny" in India, an event that also underscored the distinctiveness of certain colonized peoples and the need for special regimes to govern each of them.

50. The subject in question was a Jew of Spanish ancestry who could claim to be a British subject by virtue of his birth in Gibraltar. The case is described in Karatani, *Defining British Citizenship*, 59.

51. Sukanya Banerjee, *Becoming Imperial Citizens: Indians in the Late-Victorian Empire* (Durham, NC: Duke University Press, 2010), 17.

52. Niraja Gopal Jayal, *Citizenship and Its Discontents: An Indian History* (Cambridge, MA: Harvard University Press, 2013), 29, 30. Activists could appeal to authorities to make good on the proclamation of Queen Victoria of 1858, "We hold ourselves bound to the natives of our Indian territories by the same obligations of duty which bind us to all our other subjects. . . ." Cited in ibid., 37. Political demands came to focus both on the empire and on India as a whole, the latter a reaction to the British effort to tie its complex South Asian domain together into a single, although highly differentiated, spatial unit. Manu Goswami, *Producing India: From Colonial Economy to National Space* (Chicago: University of Chicago Press, 2004).

53. Jayal, *Citizenship and Its Discontents*, 28.

54. Ashwin Desai and Goolam Vahed, *The South African Gandhi: Stretcher-Bearer of Empire* (Stanford, CA: Stanford University Press, 2016). Desai and Vahed puncture the myth of common cause of Africans and Indians in pre-1914 South Africa, arguing that Gandhi at this time identified his people as "Aryan" and closer to Europeans than to Africans and making little effort to make common cause with the Africans suffering oppression in South Africa. Ibid., 45, 119. Some British officials in India gave mild support to the claims of Indians in South Africa. Ibid., 242–43.

55. J. E. Casely Hayford, *Gold Coast Native Institutions with Thoughts upon a Healthy Imperial Policy for the Gold Coast and Ashanti* (London: Cass, 1970 [1903]).

56. Lara Putnam, "Citizenship from the Margins: Vernacular Theories of Rights and the State from the Interwar Caribbean," *Journal of British Studies* 53 (2014): 162–91, 171 quoted, 181.

57. Dominique Colas points out that democracy "attributes sovereignty to the people, which presumes that the people is defined." That would be a big presumption in the case of the French Empire in 1789. *Citoyenneté et nationalité* (Paris: Gallimard, 2004), 11.

58. Peter Sahlins, *Unnaturally French: Foreign Citizens in the Old Regime and After* (Ithaca, NY: Cornell University Press, 2004).

59. David Bell, *The Cult of the Nation in France: Inventing Nationalism, 1680–1800* (Cambridge, MA: Harvard University Press, 2001), 51. Bell makes clear

the importance of developments in the 1740s and 1750 in articulating a sense of the nation that would then be seized upon and refashioned in the Revolution. Ibid., 10–11, 15. In putting the nation first, the good citizen was distinguishing "citizen" from "man," for the citizen might have to give up some of what he cared about as a person in order to focus loyalty on the nation. Ibid., 154.

60. See Cécile Vidal, ed., *Français? La nation en débat entre colonies et métropole, XVIe-XIXe siècle* (Paris: Éditions de l'EHESS, 2014), especially the chapters of Thomas Wien and Gilles Havard; Saliha Belmessous, "Être français en Nouvelle-France: Identité française et identité coloniale aux dix-septième et dix-huitième siècles," *French Historical Studies* 27 (2004): 507–40.

61. Richard White, *The Middle Ground: Indians, Empires, and Republics in the Great Lakes Region, 1650-1815* (Cambridge: Cambridge University Press, 1991).

62. Malick Ghachem, *The Old Regime and the Haitian Revolution* (Cambridge: Cambridge University Press, 2012).

63. This conflation of the normative and the historical is a problem, for example, in Dominique Schnapper, *La Communauté des citoyens: Sur l'idée moderne de nation* (Paris: Gallimard, 1994).

64. Michael Mann, "Ruling Class Strategies and Citizenship," in Bryan Turner and Peter Hamilton, eds., *Citizenship: Critical Concepts* (London: Routledge, 1994), 63–79.

65. The linkage of property and citizenship goes back to Roman times, particularly, according the J.G.A. Pocock, in the writing of the jurist Gaius. "The Ideal of Citizenship Since Classical Times," in Ronald Beiner, ed., *Theorizing Citizenship* (Albany: SUNY Press, 1995), 34–45.

66. Robert Castel, *From Manual Workers to Wage Laborers: Transformation of the Social Question*, trans. Richard Boyd (New Brunswick, NJ: Transaction Publishers, 2003); Mann, "Ruling Class Strategies."

67. Partha Chatterjee distinguishes the notion of citizenship from that of "population," which he considers the object of government action, producing, "a heterogeneous social, consisting of multiple population groups to be addressed through multiple and flexible policies. This was in sharp contrast with the conception of citizenship in which the insistence on the homogeneous national was both fundamental and relentless." If citizens act to defend the social and if the imperial is considered alongside the national, the dichotomy isn't so neat. *The Politics of the Governed: Reflections on Popular Politics in Most of the World* (New York: Columbia University Press, 2004), 136.

68. On the passive-active distinction, see Sahlins, *Unnaturally French*, 269–74.

69. Pierre Rosanvallon, *La société des égaux* (Paris: Seuil, 2011), 15, 22–23; Rosanvallon, *Le sacre du citoyen: Histoire du suffrage universel en France* (Paris: Gallimard, 1992), 80–81. Rosanvallon sees the demand for universal suffrage surfacing during the July Monarchy—and opening a large debate. Universal male suffrage dates to 1848. Ibid., 253, 286.

70. Overly unitary notions of citizenship are related to excessively unitary notions of sovereignty. See the thoughtful analysis in James J. Sheehan, "The Problem of Sovereignty in European History," *American Historical Review* 111 (2006): 1–15. Sheehan (3–4) conceptualizes sovereignty as a "basket" of different rights, powers, and aspirations, all components of which are the subject of claims and counterclaims.

71. The early republicans were actually rather open about welcoming their neighbors into the category of citizen. What counted, for a time, was revolutionary fervor and demonstrated loyalty. Bell, *Cult of the Nation*, 204–05.

72. On the debate over whether Saint Domingue could be considered a separate entity or as an integral part of France, and hence subject to its laws, see Maleck Ghachem, "The 'Trap' of Representation: Sovereignty, Slavery and the Road to the Haitian Revolution," *Historical Reflections/Réflexions Historiques* 29 (2003): 123–44. More generally, see the classic text of C.L.R. James, *The Black Jacobins: Toussaint L'Ouverture and the San Domingo Revolution* (New York: Vintage Books, 1963 [1938]), and the more recent book of Laurent Dubois, *Avengers of the New World: The Story of the Haitian Revolution* (Cambridge, MA: Harvard University Press, 2005). Some of the best historians and political theorists writing on France manage to exclude these issues from their consideration of the revolution's impact on citizenship.

73. Edwige Liliane Lefebvre, "Republicanism and Universalism: Factors of Inclusion or Exclusion in the French Concept of Citizenship," *Citizenship Studies* 7 (2003): 15–36, 20 quoted. Lorelle Semley provides a broad view of the relationship of citizenship to slavery, race, and colonization in French history. *To Be Free and French: Citizenship in France's Atlantic Empire* (Cambridge: Cambridge University Press, 2017).

74. Gérard Noiriel, "The Identification of the Citizen: The Birth of Republican Civil Status in France," in Jane Caplan and John Torpey, eds., *Documenting Individual Identity: The Development of State Practices in the Modern World* (Princeton, NJ: Princeton University Press, 2001), 29–30. Noiriel points out that in practice it wasn't so easy to implement the individual-state relationship, because many local officials charged with maintaining the *état civil* were illiterate or otherwise incompetent and because changing registration from a religious to a state institution was not as simple for Protestants and Jews as it was for Catholics. Under Napoleon, the *état civil* became more clearly an administrative device, less a statement of civic belonging. Ibid., 28–48.

75. Paul-André Rosental, "Civil Status and Identification in 19th Century France: A Matter of State Control?" in Keith Breckenridge and Simon Szreter, eds., *Registration and Recognition: Documenting the Person in World History* (Oxford: Oxford University Press, 2012), 137–65.

76. Laurent Dubois, *A Colony of Citizens: Revolution and Slave Emancipation in the French Caribbean, 1787–1804* (Chapel Hill: University of North Carolina Press, 2004), 254–62. The process was reversed after Napoleon reinstated slavery; slaves were now recorded only as property. While Dubois emphasizes

ex-slaves use of the new category of citizen, Ghachem (*Old Regime and the Haitian Revolution*) puts more emphasis on their use of the legal categories of the old regime in order to make claims.

77. Rebecca Scott and Michael Zeuske also demonstrate in the case of Cuba that ex-slaves often used notaries and courts to advance and to document their claims to the rights of the citizen. "Le 'droit d'avoir des droits'. Les revendications des ex-esclaves à Cuba (1872–1909)," *Annales: Histoire, Science Sociales* 59 (2004): 519–45.

78. The Civil Code, also known as the Code Napoléon, was "surely not that of political liberty," but a mechanism of authoritative regulation of the life of people worthy of "civil equality," but not of "full political and democratic citizenship." Jean-François Niort, "Sujet, citoyen et politique dans l'esprit du Code Napoléon," in Association Française des Historiens des Idées Politiques, *Sujet et Citoyen: Actes du Colloque de Lyon (11–12 septembre 2003)* (Aix-en-Provence: Presses Universitaires d'Aix-Marseille, 2004), 279–95, 285 and 294 cited.

79. There was a long debate between advocates of *jus soli* and *jus sanguinis* during the formulation of the Civil Code, eventually won (despite Napoleon's own predilections) by advocates of the latter, but with an opening to citizenship of someone born on French soil of foreign parents who remained resident and reached his majority. Luigi Lacchè, "Expanding Citizenship? The French Experience surrounding the Code Napoléon," in Clifford Ando, ed., *Citizenship and Empire in Europe 200–1900: The Antonine Constitution after 1800 Years* (Stuttgart: Franz Steiner Verlag, 2016), 177–98.

80. The most comprehensive study is Patrick Weil, *Qu'est-ce qu'un Français? Histoire de la nationalité française depuis la Révolution* (Paris: Grasset, 2002), available in English as *How to Be French: Nationality in the Making since 1789*, trans. Catherine Porter (Durham, NC: Duke University Press, 2008).

81. Silyane Larcher, *L'autre citoyen: L'idéal républicain et les Antilles après l'esclavage* (Paris: Colin, 2014), 20 quoted, 188–89, 202. Larcher notes an ambivalence on the part of ex-slaves about use of the *état civil* after the final abolition of slavery. See also Myriam Cottias, "Le silence de la nation: Les 'vieilles colonies' comme lieu de définition des dogmes républicains (1848–1905)," *Outre-Mers: Revue d'Histoire* 90, 338–39 (2003): 21–45, and Elizabeth Heath, *Wine, Sugar, and the Making of Modern France: Global Economic Crisis and the Racialization of French Citizenship, 1870–1910* (Cambridge: Cambridge University Press, 2014).

82. Naomi Andrews and Jennifer Sessions refer to the need to look beyond the "longstanding tyranny of republicanism in the historiography on France and its empire" in the nineteenth century. Amidst the ups and downs of monarchies, republics, and empires is a continuity in attempts to maintain and extend the imperial resources that France possessed. "Introduction: The Politics of Empire in Post-Revolutionary France," *French Politics, Culture and Society*, 33 (2015): 3.

83. The quotation is from Napoléon III's letter to his Governor General, 1863, http://musee.sitemestre.fr/6001/html/histoire/texte_lettre_a_pelissier.html. On status and citizenship in Algeria, see Laure Blévis, "Sociologie d'un droit colonial:

Citoyenneté et nationalité en Algérie (1865–1947): une exception républicaine?" Doctoral thesis, Institut d'Études Politiques, Université d'Aix-en-Provence-Marseille, 2004; and M'hamed Oualdi and Noureddine Amara, eds., special dossier on "La nationalité dans le monde arabe des années 1830 aux années 1960: négocier les appartenances et le droit," *Revue des mondes musulmans et de la Méditerranée* 137 (2015): 13–131.

84. Philip Nord, *The Republican Moment: Struggles for Democracy in Nineteenth-Century France* (Cambridge, MA: Harvard University Press, 1995), 252 quoted; Sudhir Hazareesingh, *From Subject to Citizen: The Second Empire and the Emergence of Modern French Democracy* (Princeton, NJ: Princeton University Press, 1998); James Lehning, *To Be a Citizen: The Political Culture of the Early French Third Republic* (Ithaca NY: Cornell University Press, 2001).

85. Emmanuelle Saada, *Empire's Children: Race, Filiation, and Citizenship in the French Colonies*, trans. Arthur Goldhammer (Chicago: University of Chicago Press, 2012). Focusing on people of mixed origins, Saada provides an insightful analysis of law, culture, status, and citizenship in the broad sweep of French history.

86. Jennifer Sessions, *By Sword and Plow: France and the Conquest of Algeria* (Ithaca, NY: Cornell University Press, 2011); Yerri Urban, *L'indigène dans le droit colonial français (1865–1955)* (Paris: Fondation Varenne, 2011); Noureddine Amara, ed., *Sous l'empire de la nationalité (1830–1960)*, special issue of *Maghreb et Sciences Sociales* 2012.

87. The constitution of the Third Republic barely mentioned colonies and did not define their place in the political structure of France or the status of the people who lived there. As Emmanuelle Saada points out, "a constitutional text from the regime of Napoleon III shaped the legal framework of the colonial possessions." Colonies, as they had been before 1789 and except for a brief period after the Revolution, were ruled by special laws or decrees. "The Absent Empire: The Colonies in French Constitutions," in Alfred McCoy, Josep Fradera, and Stephen Jacobson, eds., *Endless Empire: Spain's Retreat, Europe's Eclipse, America's Decline* (Madison: University of Wisconsin Press, 2012), 205–15, 212 quoted.

88. Blévis, "Sociologie d'un droit colonial"; Saada, *Empire's Children*.

89. Like the denial of citizenship, the indigénat provoked anxiety among some legislators and instead of having a solid statutory basis, the rules were regarded as provisional, although regularly renewed. Against the argument that a republic couldn't treat its people this way came the argument, in effect, that this is how empires were governed. Alix Héricord-Gorre, "Eléments pour une histoire de l'administration des colonisés de l'Empire français: Le 'régime de l'indigénat' et son fonctionnement depuis sa matrice algérienne (1881–c. 1920)," Doctoral thesis, European University Institute, 2008

90. Eugen Weber, *Peasants into Frenchmen: The Modernization of Rural France, 1870–1914* (Stanford, CA: Stanford University Press, 1976); Fanny Colonna, *Instituteurs algériens, 1883–1939* (Paris: Presses de la Fondation Nationales des Sciences Politiques, 1975). In general on Algeria, see Charles-Robert Ageron,

Histoire de l'Algérie contemporaine: 1830–1999 (Paris: Presses Universitaires de France, 1999) and Benjamin Stora, *Histoire de l'Algérie coloniale (1830–1954)* (Paris: La Découverte, 1991); and Daniel Rivet, *Le Maghreb à l'épreuve de la colonisation* (Paris: Fayard, 2002). Implicitly, citizenship should have opened up as subjects were acculturated through the Republic's "civilizing mission." Alice Conklin, focusing on West Africa, makes clear that republican politicians and administrators took the idea of a civilizing mission seriously, but neither devoted the resources necessary to get very far in that direction nor renounced the ideas and practices intrinsic to an imperial order. *A Mission to Civilize: The Republican Idea of Empire in France and West Africa, 1895–1930* (Stanford, CA: Stanford University Press, 1997).

91. Mamadou Diouf, "The French Colonial Policy of Assimilation and the Civility of the Originaires of the Four Communes (Senegal): A Nineteenth Century Globalization Project," *Development and Change* 29 (1998): 671–96; Hilary Jones, *The Métis of Senegal: Urban Life and Politics in French West Africa* (Bloomington: Indiana University Press, 2013); Larissa Kopytoff, "French Citizens and Muslim Law: The Tensions of Citizenship in Early Twentieth-Century Senegal," in Richard Marback and Marc W. Kruman, eds., *The Meaning of Citizenship* (Detroit: Wayne State University Press, 2015), 320–37.

92. Rebecca Shereikis writes of efforts of small communities of *originaires* from the Quatre Communes who had settled in the interior of Africa to retain their special status. But by 1913, the French government was putting them into the categories of tribe, custom, and subjecthood through which they were ruling the interior. "From Law to Custom: The Shifting Legal Status of Muslim *Originaires* in Kayes and Medine, 1903–13," *Journal of African History* 42 (2001): 261–83.

93. Elisa Camiscioli, "Producing Citizens, Reproducing the 'French Race': Immigration, Demography, and Pronatalism in Early Twentieth-Century France," *Gender and History* 13 (2001), 593–621.

94. Conklin, *Mission to Civilize*; Gregory Mann, *Native Sons: West African Veterans and France in the Twentieth Century* (Durham, NC: Duke University Press, 2006). Citizens from the Antilles also argued, eventually with success, that they should be allowed to serve France during World War I as regular soldiers. Jacques Dumont, "Conscription antillaise et citoyenneté revendiquée au tournant de la première guerre mondiale," *Vingtième Siècle* 92 (2006): 101–16. In the small French enclaves in India, there were still other variants on the relationship between status and citizenship, and they too were the basis for claim-making on the part of their original inhabitants. As people from the Indian or African enclaves moved to different parts of the empire, they took questions about their status—and the claims they could make on that basis—along with them. Natasha Pairaudeau, *Mobile Citizens: French Indians in Indochina, 1858–1954* (Copenhagen: NIAS Press, 2015); Damien Deschamps, "Une citoyenneté différée: Sens civique et assimilation des indigènes dans les Établissements français de l'Inde," *Revue Française de Science Politique* 47 (1997): 49–69.

95. The trajectory of citizenship in the Portuguese Empire in the nineteenth century is distinct from that of the Spanish, British, and French empires. Indigenous peoples were initially excluded from citizenship, in contrast to the post-1812 Spanish pattern, but some leaders pushed a more inclusive approach, which was put in place in some colonies in the face of objections to awarding citizenship to "peoples of castes and civilizations very different from our own." In the accelerating pace of colonization at the end of the century, the citizenship debate took an exclusionary turn. The *indigenato*, like the French *indigénat*, defined the subordinate place of colonized peoples in the empire. Ana Cristina Nogueira da Silva, "Universalism, Legal Pluralism and Citizenship: Portuguese Imperial Policies on Citizenship and Law (1820–1914)," in Clifford Ando, ed., *Citizenship and Empire in Europe 200–1900: The Antonine Constitution after 1800 Years* (Stuttgart: Franz Steiner Verlag, 2016), 199–220, esp. 206–17. The quotation is from a legislative debate in 1835, from ibid., 215. See also Cristina Nogueira da Silva, "Natives Who Were 'Citizens' and Natives Who Were *indígenas* in the Portuguese Empire, 1900–1926," in Alfred McCoy, Josep Fradera, and Stephen Jacobson, *Endless Empire: Spain's Retreat, Europe's Eclipse, America's Decline* (Madison: University of Wisconsin Press, 2012), 295–305.

96. Eli Nathans, *The Politics of Citizenship in Germany: Ethnicity, Utility and Nationalism* (Oxford: Berg, 2004); Geoff Eley and Jan Palmowski, eds., *Citizenship and National Identity in Twentieth-Century Germany* (Stanford, CA: Stanford University Press, 2008).

97. Dieter Gosewinkel, "Citizenship in Germany and France at the Turn of the Twentieth Century: Some New Observations on an Old Comparison," in Eley and Palmowski, *Citizenship and National Identity*, 30.

98. The population of Germany in 1871 was 41 million. Nathans, *Politics of Citizenship in Germany*, 2, 146–54. See also Annemarie Sammartino, "Culture, Belonging, and the Law: Naturalization in the Weimar Republic," in Eley and Palmowski, *Citizenship and National Identity*, 57–72.

99. Gosewinkel, 27–39; Kathleen Canning, "Reflections on the Vocabulary of Citizenship in Twentieth-Century Germany," in Eley and Palmowski, *Citizenship and National Identity*, 214–32.

100. Nathans, 201–4.

101. John Iliffe, *Tanganyika under German Rule, 1905–1912* (Cambridge: Cambridge University Press, 1969).

102. Lora Wildenthal, *German Women for Empire, 1884–1945* (Durham, NC: Duke University Press, 2001); Ann Laura Stoler, *Carnal Knowledge and Imperial Power: Race and the Intimate in Colonial Rule* (Berkeley: University of California Press, 2002).

103. George Steinmetz, *The Devil's Handwriting: Precoloniality and the German Colonial State in Qingdao, Samoa and Southwest Africa* (Chicago: University of Chicago Press, 2007).

104. Birthe Kundrus, "Colonialism, Imperialism, National Socialism: How Imperial Was the Third Reich?" in Bradley Naranch and Geoff Eley, eds., *Ger-

man Colonialism in a Global Age (Durham, NC: Duke University Press, 2014), 330–46; Sebastian Conrad, *Globalisation and the Nation in Imperial Germany* (Cambridge: Cambridge University Press, 2010); Pascal Grosse, "What Does German Colonialism Have to Do with National Socialism? A Conceptual Framework," in Eric Ames, Marcia Klotz, and Lora Wildenthal, eds., *Germany's Colonial Pasts* (Lincoln: University of Nebraska Press, 2005), 115–34; Isabelle Hull, *Absolute Destruction: Military Culture and the Practices of War in Imperial Germany* (Ithaca, NY: Cornell University Press, 2004).

105. Pieter M. Judson, *Exclusive Revolutionaries: Liberal Politics, Social Experience, and National Identity in the Austrian Empire, 1848–1914* (Ann Arbor: University of Michigan Press, 1996); Pieter M. Judson, *Guardians of the Nation: Activists on the Language Frontier of Imperial Austria* (Cambridge, MA: Harvard University Press, 2006).

106. Gérard Noiriel, *Qu'est-ce qu'une nation? Le "vivre ensemble" à la française: Réflexions d'un historien* (Montrouge: Bayard, 2015), 33; Glenda Sluga, *Internationalism in the Age of Nationalism* (Philadelphia: University of Pennsylvania Press, 2013)

107. For studies that look at the "old" multinational empires and the "new" colonial empires in relation to each other, see Jörn Leonhard and Ulrike von Hirschhausen, eds., *Comparing Empires: Encounters and Transfers in the Long Nineteenth Century* (Göttingen: Vandenhoeck & Ruprecht, 2011). The long-term but complex trajectories of imperial polities into the twentieth century is stressed in Jane Burbank and Frederick Cooper, *Empires in World History: Power and the Politics of Difference* (Princeton, NJ: Princeton University Press, 2010).

108. Engin Isin, "Citizenship after Orientalism: Ottoman Citizenship," in E. Fuat Keyman and Ahmet Içduygu, eds., *Citizenship in a Global World: European Questions and Turkish Experiences* (London: Routledge, 2005), 31–51.

109. Gianluca Parolin sees the origins of a particular citizenship doctrine in the granting of "capitulations" to foreign merchant groups in Ottoman towns, recognizing them as communities and giving them jurisdiction over legal disputes within the community. *Citizenship in the Arab World: Kin, Religion and Nation-State* (Amsterdam: Amsterdam University Press, 2009), 72.

110. Karen Barkey, *Empire of Difference: The Ottomans in Comparative Perspective* (Cambridge: Cambridge University Press, 2008); Caroline Finkel, *Osman's Dream: The History of the Ottoman Empire, 1300–1923* (New York: Basic Books, 2005); Leslie Peirce, *Imperial Harem: Women and Sovereignty in the Ottoman Empire* (New York: Oxford University Press, 1993); Leslie Peirce, *Morality Tales: Law and Gender in the Ottoman Court of Aintab* (Berkeley: University of California Press, 2003).

111. Eunjeong Yi, *Guild Dynamics in Seventeenth-Century Istanbul: Fluidity and Leverage* (Leiden: Brill, 2004), 239–40. Leslie Peirce's study of city taken over by the Ottomans suggests that local actors—some more than others— cooperated to the extent that they could gain by incorporation into the empire's

structures and networks. "Becoming Ottoman in Sixteenth-Century Aintab," in Christine Isom-Verhaaren and Kent F. Schull, Eds., *Living in the Ottoman Realm: Empire and Identity, 13th to 20th Centuries* (Bloomington: Indiana University Press, 2016), 108–22.

112. Baki Tezcan argues that the complexity of the governing structure of the Ottoman Empire, including the role of jurists, the corporate consciousness of Janissaries (and the possibility of their deposing a sultan), and the empowerment of economically successful local notables provided in the seventeenth and eighteenth centuries a check on sultanic power and an opening toward limited monarchy and some kind of civic order. The "free Muslim male" could aspire to a measure of mobility and influence. *The Second Ottoman Empire: Political and Social Transformation in the Early Modern World* (Cambridge: Cambridge University Press, 2010), 236 quoted.

113. Nora Lafi and Ulrike Freitag, eds., *Urban Governance under the Ottomans: Between Cosmopolitanism and Conflict* (London: Routledge, 2014); Sarah Abrevaya Stein, *Extraterritorial Dreams: European Citizenship, Sephardi Jews, and the Ottoman Twentieth Century* (Chicago: University of Chicago Press, 2016).

114. Will Hanley makes the case that neither the Tanzimat reforms of the 1830s nor the nationality law of 1869 defined an Ottoman citizenship. Citizenship was intended, he argues, to distinguish Ottoman subjects from foreigners and force people to choose between the protection of a foreign government and Ottoman subjecthood. He has a point—especially in that the texts in question did not provide for a set of political rights—but he limits himself to considering citizenship as a legal status (inflected by western norms concerning the political rights that citizenship *should* entail) and not as a basis of the claim-making that could stem from common membership in an Ottoman polity. "What Ottoman Nationality Was and Was Not," *Journal of the Ottoman and Turkish Studies Association* 3 (2016): 277–98.

115. Adam Mestyan finds in poetry, theater, and other creative writing from Egypt evidence of patriotic attachment to both Egypt and the Ottoman Empire. He sees patriotism as a convergence of Muslim ideas of just rule, European notions of homeland, and principles of the Ottoman imperial system. After the tendency toward autonomy in Egypt under Mehmet Ali, he sees a tendency toward "re-Ottomization." *Arab Patriotism: The Ideology and Culture of Power in Late Ottoman Egypt* (Princeton, NJ: Princeton University Press, 2017).

116. Donald Quataert, *The Ottoman Empire, 1700–1922*, 2nd ed. (Cambridge: Cambridge University Press, 2005); Barkey, *Empire of Difference*; Selim Deringil, *The Well-Protected Domains: Ideology and the Legitimation of Power in the Ottoman Empire, 1876–1909* (London: Tauris, 1998); Darin Stephanov, "Ruler Visibility, Modernity, and Ethnonationalism in the Late Ottoman Empire," in Christine Isom-Verhaaren and Kent F. Schull, eds., *Living in the Ottoman Realm: Empire and Identity, 13th to 20th Centuries* (Bloomington: Indiana University Press, 2016), 259–71.

117. Lâle Can points to the tension between the Ottoman emperor as sultan, ruler of a territorial and multi-faith empire that existed among other territorial empires, and as caliph, leader of the faithful wherever they were. The tension was strong near the edges of the empire and among people who moved across those edges, notably people from Central Asia who fell between the imperial jurisdictions of the Ottoman and Russian empires. "The Protection Question: Central Asians and Extraterritoriality in the Late Ottoman Empire," *International Journal of Middle East Studies* 48 (2016): 679–99, esp. 692. On sectarian tensions in Ottoman Lebanon, see Ussama Makdisi, *The Culture of Sectarianism: Community, History, and Violence in Nineteenth-Century Ottoman Lebanon* (Berkeley: University of California Press, 2000).

118. Ali Yaycioglu, *Partners of the Empire: The Crisis of the Ottoman Order in the Age of Revolutions* (Stanford, CA: Stanford University Press, 2016), 2–4.

119. Ottoman attempts to make governing practices more standard for the different religions—at a time when coreligionists from other empires were meddling—exacerbated sectarian tendencies in mid-nineteenth-century Lebanon. Makdisi, *The Culture of Sectarianism*.

120. Thomas Kuehn, "Shaping and Reshaping Colonial Ottomanism: Contesting Boundaries of Difference and Integration in Ottoman Yemen, 1872–1919," *Comparative Studies of South Asia, Africa, and the Middle East* 27 (2007): 315–31, 317 quoted. Thomas Kuehn, *Empire, Islam, and Politics of Difference: Ottoman Rule in Yemen, 1849–1919* (Leiden: Brill, 2011). Kuehn compares Ottoman rule in Yemen—but not in more central provinces of the empire—to British practices of indirect rule. Ibid., 251.

121. Michelle Campos, *Ottoman Brothers: Muslims, Christians, and Jews in Early Twentieth-Century Palestine* (Stanford, CA: Stanford University Press, 2010); Julia Phillips Cohen, *Becoming Ottomans: Sephardi Jews and Imperial Citizenship in the Modern Era* (New York: Oxford University Press, 2014); Will Hanley, "When Did Egyptians Stop Being Ottomans? An Imperial Citizenship Case Study," in Willem Maas, ed. *Multilevel Citizenship* (Philadelphia: University of Pennsylvania Press, 2013), 89–109; Ariel Salzmann, "Citizens in Search of the State: The Limits of Political Participation in the Late Ottoman Empire," in Michael Hanagan and Charles Tilly, eds., *Extending Citizenship, Reconfiguring States* (New York: Rowman and Littlefield, 1999), 37–66.

122. Nicholas Doumanis, *Before the Nation: Muslim-Christian Coexistence and Its Destruction in Late-Ottoman Anatolia* (Oxford: Oxford University Press, 2013). The Greek nationalists who fought for independence from the Ottoman Empire in the 1820s got considerable help from European powers that wanted to limit the power of the Ottomans, and the first king of Greece was actually a Bavarian prince. If Britain and France wanted to weaken the Ottomans, they didn't want to weaken them too much, and later tried to play the Ottomans off against the Russians. The conflicts of the Mediterranean world in the nineteenth century are not simply struggles of nations against empires, but inter-empire conflict and intrigue.

123. Laura Robson, *States of Separation: Transfer, Partition, and the Making of the Modern Middle East* (Berkeley: University of California Press, 2017), 21–24.

124. See Doumanis, *Before the Nation*, 132–69.

125. Ronald Grigor Suny, Fatma Müge Göçek, and Norman M Naimark, eds., *A Question of Genocide: Armenians and Turks at the End of the Ottoman Empire* (Oxford: Oxford University Press, 2011); Philipp Ther, *The Dark Side of Nation-States: Ethnic Cleansing in Modern Europe* (London: Berghahn, 2014). Christopher Bayly stresses the importance of the war itself in pushing the governing elite into a nationalist mode. Up to that point, he writes citing Engin Akarli and Hasan Kayali, "Young Turks were essentially Ottoman patriots, not harbingers of a Turkish ethnic state." "Distorted Development: The Ottoman Empire and British India, circa 1780–1916," *Comparative Studies of South Asia, Africa, and the Middle East* 27 (2007): 332–34, 334 quoted.

126. Hasan Kayali, *Arabs and Young Turks: Ottomanism, Arabism, and Islamism in the Ottoman Empire, 1908–1918* (Berkeley: University of California Press, 1997). Jürgen Osterhammel points out that in the final years of the Ottoman Empire, the challenge "did not come from disgruntled minority elites or oppressed peasantries but from the margins of the military establishment." He makes much the same point about the other "old" empires in the early twentieth century. "Commentary: Measuring Imperial 'Success' and 'Failure,'" in Leonhard and von Hirschhausen, *Comparing Empires*, 472–76, 473 quoted.

127. Like citizenship in the Ottoman Empire, the question of forms of political belonging in China—in relation to the long history of empire and to European intrusion—has received scholarly attention and deserves more. See Merle Goldman and Elizabeth Perry, eds., *Changing Meanings of Citizenship in Modern China* (Cambridge, MA: Harvard University Press, 2002); Joshua Fogel and Peter Zarrow, eds., *Imagining the People: Chinese Intellectuals and the Concept of Citizenship, 1890–1920* (Armonk, NY: M. E. Sharpe, 1997); Vanessa Fong and Rachel Murphy, eds., *Chinese Citizenship: Views from the Margins* (London: Routledge, 2006); "Symposium: 'Public Sphere'/'Civil Society' in China?," *Modern China* 19, 2 (1993); R. Bin Wong, "Citizenship in Chinese History," in Michael Hanagan and Charles Tilly, eds., *Extending Citizenship, Reconfiguring States* (Lanham, MD: Rowman and Littlefield, 1999), 97–122. Citizenship in African polities will be discussed in chapter 3.

128. Peter Baldwin, *The Politics of Social Solidarity Class Bases of the European Welfare State, 1875–1975* (Cambridge: Cambridge University Press, 1992). See also Castel, *From Manual Workers to Wage Laborers*.

129. John Torpey, *The Invention of the Passport: Surveillance, Citizenship, and the State* (Cambridge: Cambridge University Press, 2000).

130. Paul-André Rosental, "National Citizenship and Migrants' Social Rights in Twentieth-Century Europe," in Steven King and Anne Winter, eds., *Migration, Settlement and Belonging in Europe, 1500–1930s* (Oxford: Berghahn Books,

2013), 269–80; Mary Dewhurst Lewis, *The Boundaries of the Republic: Migrant Rights and the Limits of Universalism in France, 1918–1940* (Stanford, CA: Stanford University Press, 2007). McKeown makes a related point regarding Chinese immigrants to the United States: many found that there were ways, legal and otherwise, to evade the restrictions. *Melancholy Order*, 273.

131. Paul Kramer, *The Blood of Government: Race, Empire, the United States, and the Philippines* (Chapel Hill: University of North Carolina Press, 2006).

132. Aihwa Ong, *Flexible Citizenship: The Cultural Logics of Transnationality* (Durham, NC: Duke University Press, 1999).

Chapter 3. Empires, Nations, and Citizenship in the Twentieth Century

1. Hannah Arendt, *The Origins of Totalitarianism*, new ed. (New York: Harcourt Brace 1979 [1948]), 290–302. On contemporary anxieties about *apatrides*, see for example Nicolas Weill, "L'apatridie, l'envers du droit," *Le Monde* 14 January 2016.

2. Rogers Brubaker, *Nationalism Reframed: Nationhood and the National Question in the New Europe* (Cambridge: Cambridge University Press, 1996); Philipp Ther, *The Dark Side of Nation-States: Ethnic Cleansing in Modern Europe* (London: Berghahn, 2014); Jessica Reinisch and Elizabeth White, eds., *The Disentanglement of Populations: Migration, Expulsion and Displacement in Postwar Europe, 1944–49* (London: Palgrave Macmillan, 2011).

3. Laura Robson, *States of Separation: Transfer, Partition, and the Making of the Modern Middle East* (Berkeley: University of California Press, 2017); Eric Weitz, "Self-Determination: How a German Enlightenment Idea Became the Slogan of National Liberation and a Human Right," *American Historical Review* 120 (2015): 462–96.

4. Niraja Gopal Jayal, *Citizenship and Its Discontents: An Indian History* (Cambridge, MA: Harvard University Press, 2013), 31–32.

5. Jayal sees imperial citizenship as differentiated by racial hierarchy, while the colonial framework—within India—was differentiated both by race and by class. Ibid., 29.

6. The tensions between gender, community, and nation are emphasized in Mrinalini Sinha, *Specters of Mother India: The Global Restructuring of an Empire* (Durham, NC: Duke University Press, 2006).

7. Sandip Hazareesingh, "The Quest for Urban Citizenship: Civic Rights, Public Opinion, and Colonial Resistance in Early Twentieth-Century Bombay," *Modern Asian Studies* 34 (2000): 797–829.

8. Jayal, *Citizenship and Its Discontents*, 41, 44.

9. Smuts, 1921, quoted in Mrinalini Sinha, "Whatever Happened to the Third British Empire? Empire, Nation Redux," in Andrew Thompson, ed., *Writing Imperial Histories* (Manchester: Manchester University Press, 2013), 180.

10. Sunil Amrith, "Empires, Diasporas and Cultural Circulation," in Andrew Thompson, ed., *Writing Imperial Histories* (Manchester: Manchester University Press, 2013), 232.

11. Sinha, *Specters of Mother India.*

12. Jayal, *Citizenship and Its Discontents,* 19, 22, 162 quoted.

13. Md. Mahbubar Rahman and Willem Van Schendel argue that cross-border refugee movements at partition were of different types and not all migrants were refugees. "'I Am Not a Refugee': Rethinking Partition Migration," *Modern Asian Studies* 37 (2003): 551–84.

14. Joya Chatterji, "South Asian Histories of Citizenship, 1946–1970," *The Historical Journal* 55 (2012): 1049–71, 1070 quoted. Chatterji's characterization is a response to Aihwa Ong, *Flexible Citizenship: The Cultural Logics of Transnationality* (Durham NC: Duke University Press, 1999). Chatterji also notes that "Today South Asia's borders are among the most violently policed frontiers in the world." That other former colonies around the Indian Ocean became independent in the postwar period led to exclusionary tendencies toward the many South Asians living there, while India's desire to retain ties with its diaspora were mitigated by concerns that closet Pakistanis might infiltrate the mother country. "From Subject to Citizen: Migration, Nationality, and the Post-imperial Global Order," in Alfred McCoy, Josep Fradera, and Stephen Jacobson, eds., *Endless Empire: Spain's Retreat, Europe's Eclipse, America's Decline* (Madison: University of Wisconsin Press, 2012), 311–12.

15. Seyla Benhabib, *The Rights of Others: Aliens, Residents and Citizens* (Cambridge: Cambridge University Press, 2004).

16. In the 1930s, the convergence of critical intellectuals and activists on London from around the British Empire led to a considerable range of anti-colonial activities, not least among them a demand for a meaningful form of imperial citizenship. Marc Matera, *Black London: The Imperial Metropolis and Decolonization in the Twentieth Century* (Berkeley: University of California Press, 2015).

17. A. G. Hopkins, "Rethinking Decolonization," *Past and Present* 200 (2008): 211–47.

18. Randall Hansen, "The Politics of Citizenship in 1940s Britain: The British Nationality Act," *Twentieth Century British History* 10 (1999): 67–95.

19. Randall Hansen, *Citizenship and Immigration in Post-War Britain: The Institutional Origins of a Multicultural Nation* (Oxford: Oxford University Press, 2000), 245–47, 251.

20. Matthew Grant, "Historicizing Citizenship in Post-War Britain," *The Historical Journal* 59 (2016): 1187–1206. As Hansen (*Citizenship and Immigration,* 252) points out, even earlier the Nationality Act's original purpose of maintaining the cohesion of the Commonwealth through an inclusive citizenship regime was undermined not only by the attitudes of some of Britain's "white" citizens, but by both ends of the overseas spectrum—by old dominions that wanted to restrict nonwhite immigration and by newly independent states

that wanted to assert their autonomy and define their own citizenships. See also Sarah Ansari, "Subjects or Citizens?" India, Pakistan and the 1948 British Nationality Act," *Journal of Imperial and Commonwealth History* 41 (2013): 285–312; Kathleen Paul, *Whitewashing Britain: Race and Citizenship in the Postwar Era* (Ithaca, NY: Cornell University Press, 1997); and Chatterji, "From Subject to Citizen," 315.

21. Jane Burbank, "Eurasian Sovereignty: The Case of Kazan," *Problems of Post-Communism* 62 (2015): 8.

22. Valerie Kivelson, " 'Muscovite Citizenship': Rights without Freedom," *Journal of Modern History* 74 (2002): 465–89.

23. Charles Steinwedel, "Making Social Groups, One Person at a Time: The Identification of Individuals, by Estate, Religious Confession, and Ethnicity in Late Imperial Russia," in Jane Caplan and John Torpey, eds., *Documenting Individual Identity: The Development of State Practices in the Modern World* (Princeton, NJ: Princeton University Press, 2001), 67–82. Registers and internal passports were used to control residence and movement (whether to encourage or discourage it depending on the needs of the state). Steinwedel points out the "nationality" was considered more of a long-term attribute than religion or estate, but was neither racial nor rigid. Ibid., 82.

24. Eric Lohr, *Russian Citizenship from Empire to Soviet Union* (Cambridge, MA: Harvard University Press, 2012), 32; Paul Werth, *the Tsar's Foreign Faiths: Toleration and the Fate of Religious Freedom in Imperial Russia* (Oxford: Oxford University Press, 2014). There was nothing unusual about the fact that with the incorporation of Finland into the empire, Finns retained their own form of citizenship with a fuller range of rights than enjoyed by most Russians. Such were the imperatives of incorporative imperialism. Lohr, *Russian Citizenship*, 30–31. For a debate on Lohr's arguments, see Andrey Shlyakhter, "Russian Citizenship: Borders, Numbers and Intentions," Russian History Blog, http:// russianhistoryblog.org/2013/07/russian-citizenship-borders-numbers-and-in tentions-3/, accessed January 12, 2016, plus comments, including Lohr's reply. The arguments cited in these passages are not fundamentally challenged by Shlyakhter's critique.

25. Lohr (*Russian Citizenship*, 5) refers to this policy as "attract and hold." The exception to low rates of emigration were Jews. The government did not discourage them from leaving and made it hard for Jews who left ever to return. Ibid., 113.

26. Jane Burbank, "An Imperial Rights Regime: Law and Citizenship in the Russian Empire," *Kritika: Explorations in Russian and Eurasian History* 7 (2006): 397–431; Lohr, *Russian Citizenship*, 3.

27. Lohr, *Russian Citizenship*, 72, 79–80.

28. Ibid., 130.

29. Ibid., 131–34.

30. The Soviet model of national republics was influential beyond its borders. It was cited in 1946 as a precedent for turning the French Empire into a

federation and in 1995 for turning the unitary state of Ethiopia into a federal state—cases to be discussed later in this chapter. Christopher Clapham, "Afterword," in David Turton, ed., *Ethnic Federalism: The Ethiopian Experience in Comparative Perspective* (Oxford: James Currey, 2006), 237.

31. Lohr (*Russian Citizenship*, 156) cites a statute from 1924: "The citizen of one of the union republics within the composition of the USSR is at the same time a citizen of the USSR and possesses all the rights and carries all the obligations established by the constitution and laws of the USSR as well as by the constitution and laws of the Soviet republic in which he resides." See also Francine Hirsch, *Empire of Nations: Ethnographic Knowledge and the Making of the Soviet Union* (Ithaca, NY: Cornell University Press, 2005); Terry Martin, *The Affirmative Action Empire: Nations and Nationalism in the Soviet Union, 1923–1939* (Ithaca, NY: Cornell University Press, 2001).

32. The internal passport became an instrument of control, used against individuals or communities whose actions or attitudes were suspect, confining some to exile or labor camps, but also doling out access to resources depending on social position. Marc Garcelon, "Colonizing the Subject: The Genealogy and Legacy of the Soviet Internal Passport," in Jane Caplan and John Torpey, eds., *Documenting Individual Identity: The Development of State Practices in the Modern World* (Princeton, NJ: Princeton University Press, 2001), 83–100.

33. Vanessa Ruget, "Citizenship in Central Asia," in Peter Nyers and Engin Isin, eds., *The Routledge Handbook of Global Citizenship Studies* (London: Routledge, 2015), 335–43.

34. Lohr, *Russian Citizenship*, 186.

35. Sally Cummings and Raymond Hinnebusch, "Introduction," in Cummings and Hinnebusch, eds., *Sovereignty after Empire: Comparing the Middle East and Central Asia* (Edinburgh: University of Edinburgh Press, 2011), 4. They argue that the Middle East was fragmented by the imposed borders but harked back to memories of Islamic unity under the Ottoman Empire and earlier Islamic empires ("Conclusions," 335). The twentieth century brought in new forms of social fragmentation—old and new urban elites, rural landowners, military elites of more modest origin, wage workers, peasants with marginal access to resources—as well as a variety of Islamic beliefs and networks. The consequence was governing classes with little legitimacy, and governed classes with high levels of resentment against both outsiders and rulers.

36. Susan Pedersen, *The Guardians: The League of Nations and the Crisis of Empire* (New York: Oxford University Press; Natasha Wheatley, "Mandatory Interpretation: Legal Hermeneutics and the New International Order in Arab and Jewish Petitions to the League of Nations," *Past and Present*, 227 (2015): 205–48.

37. Cummings and Hinnebusch, "Introduction," 1–22, and "Conclusion," 337 cited, in Cummings and Hinnebusch, *Sovereignty after Empire*.

38. Emmanuelle Saada, *Empire's Children: Race, Filiation, and Citizenship in the French Colonies*, trans. Arthur Goldhammer (Chicago: University of Chicago Press, 2012).

39. Emir Khaled's real name was Khaled El-Hassani Ben El-Hachem, and he was the grandson of the resistance leader Abd El-Khader and an officer in the French Army during World War I.

40. Dónal Hassett, "Defining Imperial Citizenship in the Shadow of World War I: Equality and Difference in the Debates around Post-Colonial Reform in Algeria," in Gearóid Barry, Enrico Dal Lago, and Róisín Healy, eds., *Small Nations and Colonial Peripheries in World War I* (Leiden: Brill, 2016), 263–80. Other French politicians argued (also to no avail) for creating a "demi-citoyenneté" that allowed Muslims to exercise certain rights, or that limited political rights could be extended to noncitizens, kept carefully segregated from the citizen-electorate. Florence Renucci, "L'accession des indigènes à la citoyenneté entre assimilation et réformisme: Les mesures légales prises par l'Italie et la France en 1919," in Association Française des Historiens des Idées Politiques, *Sujet et Citoyen: Actes du Colloque de Lyon (11–12 septembre 2003)* (Aix-en-Provence: Presses Universitaires d'Aix-Marseille, 2004), 393–420.

41. James McDougall, *History and the Culture of Nationalism in Algeria* (Cambridge: Cambridge University Press, 2006). Yet another pattern prevailed in the mandates that France acquired over the former Ottoman provinces of Syria and Lebanon. Elizabeth Thompson points to the grey area between the status of subject and citizen, and to the tensions over social relations, including gender and class—in short, the specific nature of citizenship—that emerged as claims to rights were made. *Colonial Citizens: Republican Rights, Paternal Privilege, and Gender in French Syria and Lebanon* (New York: Columbia University Press, 2000).

42. Gary Wilder, *Freedom Time: Negritude, Decolonization, and the Future of the World* (Durham, NC: Duke University Press, 2015). Like London, Paris was where intellectuals and activists from around the empire converged, under-scoring the shared anger at the exclusions of French citizenship. Whether such trends can be fit into a narrative of nationalism or whether the other threads deserve full consideration in their own right is a matter of controversy among historians. For two points of view, see Michael Goebel, *Anti-imperial Metropolis: Interwar Paris and the Seeds of Third-world Nationalism* (Cambridge: Cambridge University Press, 2016), and Jennifer Boittin, *Colonial Metropolis: The Urban Grounds of Anti-imperialism and Feminism in Interwar Paris* (Lincoln: University of Nebraska Press, 2010).

43. This and the following paragraphs are based on a more detailed discussion of the 1946 constitution and the reconfiguration of citizenship in Frederick Cooper, *Citizenship between Empire and Nation: Remaking France and French Africa, 1945–1960* (Princeton, NJ: Princeton University Press, 2014).

44. According to French officials, some men in the French Sudan complained that women's equal access to courts under the citizenship clauses had undermined their marital authority. In 1947 the administration of that territory issued a decree that reinstated the former practice of imposing criminal sanctions on women who had deserted the marital home, but applied the decree only

to women married under customary law, not the French civil code. Marie Rodet, "Continuum of Gendered Violence: The Colonial Invention of Female Desertion as a Customary Criminal Offense, French Soudan, 1900–1949," in Emily Burrill, Richard Roberts, and Elizabeth Thornberry, eds., *Domestic Violence and the Law in Colonial and Postcolonial Africa* (Athens: Ohio University Press, 2010), 86.

45. Technically, citizenship of the French Union embraced everybody, but it meant little for citizens of the French Republic, including overseas territories and Algeria, because they had something better. Union citizenship was thus meaningful for inhabitants of protectorates and to a lesser extent mandates, because the government, following League of Nations precedents, accepted that the inhabitants of mandated territories had to be treated at least as well as those of colonies or overseas territories. Just what Union citizenship provided was not so clear, since implementation presumably went through the individual governments, and the monarchs who nominally ruled Morocco, Tunisia, or Vietnam did not necessarily accept republican notions of citizenship. For a leading jurist's take on citizenship of the French Union, see Pierre Lampué, "L'Union Française d'après la Constitution," *Revue Juridique et Parlementaire de l'Union Française*, 1 (1947), 1–39, 145–94.

46. Kristen Stromberg Childers, *Seeking Imperialism's Embrace: National Identity, Decolonization, and Assimilation in the French Caribbean* (New York: Oxford University Press, 2016).

47. Much too late, the French government—alongside its brutal repression of the Algerian revolt—tried to play the "integration" card to Muslim Algerians, including a program of what Americans would call affirmative action, guaranteeing "French Muslim Algerians" a percentage of civil service jobs in the metropole as well as in Algeria itself. The premise of the failed campaign was that France was an inclusive and differentiated polity and could act—or should be seen to act—for the benefit of particular categories of its citizens. Todd Shepard, "Thinking between Metropole and Colony: The French Republic, 'Exceptional Promotion,' and the 'Integration' of Algerians, 1955–1962," in Martin Thomas, ed., *The French Colonial Mind*, vol. 1: *Mental Maps of Empire and Colonial Encounters* (Lincoln: University of Nebraska Press, 2012), 298–323.

48. For the different pattern of making citizenship claims in the context of the welfare state in 1940s Lebanon and Syria, see Thompson, *Colonial Citizens*.

49. Sékou Touré and Houphouët-Boigny both wanted Africa to remain in the "Franco-African Community," but the former favored an African federation, the latter opposed it.

50. Willem Maas, ed., *Multilevel Citizenship* (Philadelphia: University of Pennsylvania, 2013).

51. The French overseas territory of the Sudan—now the Republic of Mali—should not be confused with the state that now bears the name of Sudan.

52. Benhabib writes that "Not having one's papers in order in our societies is a form of civil death." *Rights of Others*, 215.

53. The distinguished Franco-Iranian sociologist Farhad Khosrokhovar points out that France promised its Muslim citizens equal opportunity and delivered stigmatization, leading to a higher level of bitterness than is found in Germany or England. "Laïcité," he writes, "France's staunch version of secularism, is so inflexible that it can appear to rob them of dignity." "Jihad and the French Exception," *New York Times*, July 19, 2016.

54. The possibility of being a citizen with a particular civil status still exists, for now at least, in New Caledonia. See among a growing body of work Isabelle Merle and Elsa Faugère, eds., *La Nouvelle-Calédonie: Vers un destin commun* (Paris: Karthala, 2010).

55. On the complexities of laws on citizenship and nationality in past and present, see Patrick Weil, *Qu'est-ce qu'un Français? Histoire de la nationalité française depuis la Révolution* (Paris: Grasset, 2005).

56. Some places to begin are Sara Dorman, "Citizenship in Africa: The Politics of Belonging," in Engin Isin and Peter Nyers, eds., *The Routledge Handbook of Global Citizenship Studies* (London: Routledge, 2015), 161-71; Emma Hunter, ed., *Citizenship, Belonging, and Political Community in Africa: Dialogues between Past and Present* (Athens: Ohio University Press, 2016); and Edmond Keller, *Identity, Citizenship, and Political Conflict in Africa* (Bloomington: Indiana University Press, 2014). On how African states developed nationality laws after independence, see Roger Decottignies and Marc de Biéville, *Les nationalités africaines* (Paris: Pedone, 1963).

57. Mamadou Diouf and Rosalind Fredericks, eds., *The Arts of Citizenship in African Cities: Infrastructures and Spaces of Belonging* (London: Palgrave Macmillan, 2014).

58. Sten Hagberg, "'Thousands of New Sankaras': Resistance and Struggle in Burkina Faso," *Africa Spectrum* 3 (2015): 109-21.

59. Richard Banégas, Florence Brisset-Foucault, and Armando Cutolo, "Espaces publics de la parole et pratiques de la citoyenneté en Afrique," *Politique africaine* 127 (2012): 5-20.

60. Blair Rutherford, "On the Promise and Perils of Citizenship: Heuristic Concepts, Zimbabwean Example," *Citizenship Studies* 15 (2011): 499-512.

61. Laurent Fourchard and Aurelia Segatti, "Of Xenophobia and Citizenship: The Everyday Politics of Exclusion and Inclusion in Africa," *Africa* 85 (2015): 2-12; Jonathan Klaaren, "Citizenship, Xenophobic Violence, and Law's Dark Side," in Loren Landau, ed., *Exorcising The Demon Within: Xenophobia, Violence, and Statecraft in Contemporary South Africa* (Johannesburg: Wits University Press, 2010), 135-49; Audie Klotz, *Migration and National Identity in South Africa, 1860-2010* (Cambridge: Cambridge University Press, 2013); Tamlyn Monson, "Everyday Politics and Collective Mobilization against Foreigners in a South African Shack Settlement," *Africa* 85 (2015): 131-53. The South African government has stated that all South Africans, regardless of race, are full citizens. That has not been the case everywhere in post-independence Africa. In much of East Africa, for instance, not just people of European origin

but those with South Asian roots were the target of efforts to define them as less than full citizens of Tanganyika, Uganda, or (to a lesser extent) Kenya. Many had to leave a country in which they had been brought up. On race and citizenship in the case of Tanganyika (later Tanzania), see Ronald Aminzade, "The Politics of Race and Nation: Citizenship and Africanization in Tanganyika," *Political Power and Social Theory* 14 (2000): 53–90; and James Brennan, *Taifa: Making Nation and Race in Urban Tanzania* (Athens: Ohio University Press, 2012).

62. The following paragraphs are based on Henri-Michel Yéré, "Citizenship, Nationality and History in Côte d'Ivoire, 1929–1999," Ph.D. dissertation, University of Basel, 2010; Peter Geschiere, *The Perils of Belonging: Autochthony, Citizenship, and Exclusion in Africa and Europe* (Chicago: University of Chicago Press, 2009); Ruth Marshall-Fratani, "The War of 'Who Is Who': Autochthony, Nationalism, and Citizenship in the Ivorian Crisis," *African Studies Review* 49 (2006): 9–43; as well as Cooper, *Citizenship between Empire and Nation*.

63. Political scientist Lauren MacLean found that citizenship structures make considerable difference at a local level. Comparing villages of similar ethnic composition on both sides of the Côte d'Ivoire-Ghana border, she found that the strong notion of citizenship inherited from post-1946 France, and which continued to shape electoral politics and service delivery under Houphouët-Boigny fostered among Ivorians a more "individualized, entitlement-based sense of citizenship" and greater focus on the nuclear family than their Ghanaian cousins, who had developed a wider sense of their local community in the face of the state's failure since the 1960s to provide much of anything in the way of social services to its citizens. *Informal Institutions and Citizenship in Rural Africa: Risk and Reciprocity in Ghana and Côte d'Ivoire* (Cambridge: Cambridge University Press, 2010), 6 quoted.

64. A similar situation prevailed in Zimbabwe in the early 2000s: government edicts purging from citizenship roles people with connections (usually as migrant workers) to another state and questioning the status of urban dwellers on the grounds that the true Zimbabwe citizen was attached to the land. In effect, the true Zimbabwean citizen was someone who supported the government party. Dorman, "Citizenship in Africa"; Shannon Morreira, *Rights after Wrongs: Local Knowledge and Human Rights in Zimbabwe* (Stanford, CA: Stanford University Press, 2016), 17–19.

65. Thandika Mkandawire, "African Intellectuals and Nationalism," in Mkandawire, ed., *African Intellectuals: Rethinking Politics, Language, Gender and Development* (Dakar: CODESRIA; London: Zed, 2005), 12. See also Sara Dorman, Daniel Hammett, and Paul Nugent, "Introduction: Citizenship and Its Casualties in Africa," in Dorman, Hammet, and Nugent, eds., *Making Nations, Creating Strangers: States and Citizenship in Africa* (Leiden: Brill, 2007), 3–26, and Beth Elise Whitaker, "Citizens and Foreigners: Democratization and the Politics of Exclusion in Africa" *African Studies Review* 48 (2005): 109–26.

66. Carola Lentz, *Land, Mobility, and Belonging in West Africa* (Bloomington: Indiana University Press, 2013), 2. See also Paul Bjerk, "The Allocation of

Land as a Historical Discourse of Political Authority in Tanzania," *International Journal of African Historical Studies* 46 (2013): 255–82; Bjerk notes the changing levels of authority—from kinship group to chiefs to the Tanzanian state—that intervene in the allocation of land.

67. Catherine Boone, *Property and Political Order in Africa: Land Rights and the Structure of Politics* (Cambridge: Cambridge University Press, 2014), 313.

68. Christian Lund, "Proprieté et citoyenneté: Dynamiques de reconnaissance dans l'Afrique des villes," *Politique africaine* 132 (2013): 5–25. For a study of status and gender oppression in parts of rural Africa, see Benedetta Rossi, *From Slavery to Aid: Politics, Labour, and Ecology in the Nigerien Sahel, 1800–2000* (Cambridge: Cambridge University Press, 2015). One response to government hostility in rural Guinea has been migration to Senegal. John Straussberger, "The 'Particular Situation' in the Futa Jallon: Ethnicity, Region, and Nation in Twentieth-Century Guinea," PhD dissertation, Columbia University, 2015.

69. Vasco Martins, "Politics of Power and Hierarchies of Citizenship in Angola," *Citizenship Studies* 21 (2017): 100–15; Justin Pearce, *Political Identity and Conflict in Central Angola, 1975–2002* (Cambridge: Cambridge University Press, 2015).

70. Aninka Claassens, "Denying Ownership and Equal Citizenship: Continuities in the State's Use of Law and 'Custom'", 1913–2013," *Journal of Southern African Studies* 40 (2014): 761–779, 774 quoted; Deborah James, "Citzenship and Land in South Africa: From Rights to Responsibilities," *Critique of Anthropology* 33 (2013): 26–46. To take a quite different African example, among the countries of the Chad Basin people act not only in relation to those states, but in relation to transborder networks of different sorts—smuggling arms, drugs, and household goods—each of which offers a sense of belonging as well as material—often violent—support, regulates commercial interaction, and "taxes" resources. People have to operate in this complex field of state and non-state institutions that are not entirely distinct from each other. Janet Roitman, "The Right to Tax: Economic Citizenship in the Chad Basin," *Citizenship Studies* 11 (2007): 187–209.

71. Long ago, Aristide Zolberg pointed out that African political parties were less mass organizations than assemblages put together by leaders working through vertical linkages to brokers in each of the ethnic communities, religious groupings, or associations of various sorts that constituted society, more like the political structures of political bosses in Chicago than the mass party of Leninist imagination. *Creating Political Order: The Party States of West Africa* (Chicago: Rand-McNally, 1966). My (and Zolberg's) perspective differs from arguments that posit a sharp bifurcation between a world of cities, formal political organization, and citizenship versus a rural world of kinship and kin-like ties and, in the colonial era, subjecthood. Mahmood Mamdani, *Citizen and Subject: Contemporary Africa and the Legacy of Late Colonialism* (Princeton, NJ: Princeton University Press, 1996), and Peter Ekeh, "Colonialism and the Two Publics in Africa: A Theoretical Statement," *Comparative Studies in Society and History* 17 (1975): 91–112.

72. For a study of how extreme differentiation—in relation to people of slave status—in an earlier time period plays out in the context of both urbanization and the development of a state-defined national citizenship, see Éric Hahonou, "Propriété, citoyennetés et héritage de l'esclavage au Nord Bénin," *Politique Africaine* 132 (2013): 73–93.

73. These tendencies are emphasized in John Lonsdale, "Unhelpful Pasts and a Provisional Present," in Hunter, *Citizenship, Belonging, and Political Community in Africa*, chapter 2. Movement to cities created possibilities for people to claim human and material resources in new ways, but also the possibility of control of such resources by elites. That urban societies are "plural" in many senses—different origins, different notions of law and property, different relations to political parties and state institutions—makes the question of urban citizenship all the more complex. See Lund, "Proprieté et citoyenneté," 5–25.

74. Juan Obarrio, *The Spirit of the Laws in Mozambique* (Chicago: University of Chicago Press, 2014), 6 quoted; Elisio Macamo, "Power, Conflict, and Citizenship: Mozambique's Contemporary Struggles," *Citizenship Studies* 21 (2017): 196–209, 198 quoted; Jason Hickel, *Democracy as Death: The Moral Order of Anti-Liberal Politics in South Africa* (Berkeley: University of California Press, 2015), 23 quoted.

75. Steven Robins, Andrea Cornwall and Bettina von Lieres, "Rethinking 'Citizenship' in the Postcolony," *Third World Quarterly* 29 (2008): 1069–86. A related, equally problematic, argument appears in Patrick Chabal and Jean-Pascal Deloz, *Africa Works: Disorder as Political Instrument* (Bloomington: Indiana University Press, 1999).

76. Harri Englund, "Introduction: Recognizing Identities, Imagining Alternatives," in Englund and Francis B. Nyamnjoh, eds., *Rights and the Politics of Recognition in Africa* (London: Zed, 2004), 23. "Groups" are to differing degrees constituted out of long-standing patterns of belonging, but also from the efforts of political elites and entrepreneurs of cultural particularity. For an example of "top-down" group-based citizenship, see Helene Maria Kyed, "New Sites of Citizenship: Recognition of Traditional Authority and Group-based Citizenship in Mozambique," *Journal of Southern African Studies* 32 (2006): 563–81.

77. Remittances from Africans abroad to African countries were around $35–36 billion in 2015. "Remittances to Developing Countries Edge Up Slightly in 2015," worldbank.org, accessed November 22, 2016. The concept of diasporic citizenship is discussed in the introduction.

78. Lahra Smith, *Making Citizens in Africa: Ethnicity, Gender and National Identity in Ethiopia* (Cambridge: Cambridge University Press, 2013), 6, 204 quoted; David Turton, "Introduction," in Turton, ed., *Ethnic Federalism: The Ethiopian Experience in Comparative Perspective* (Oxford: James Currey, 2006), 14, 18; Assefa Fiseha, "Theory versus Practice in the Implementation of Ethiopia's Ethnic Federalism," in Turton, *Ethnic Federalism*, 131–64. Solomon M. Gofie argues that the state used pluralistic notion of a community of citizens to cement its monolithic approach to political power. "The State and the 'Peoples':

Citizenship and the Future of Political Community in Ethiopia," in Emma Hunter, ed., *Citizenship, Belonging, and Political Community in Africa: Dialogues between Past and Present* (Athens: Ohio University Press, 2016), 240–55. A mixed picture of postcolonial federalism also emerges in Nigeria. Following the British-constructed division of Nigeria into three units was a predictable disaster, as each risked domination by an alliance of the other two, and the largest ethnic group in each was in a position to make the entire region conform to its dictates. After the Biafran war of 1967–70, the country was divided into a larger number of federated states (later increased again), complicating the quest for ethnic domination both within and among the states. There has been no repeat of the Biafran war, although the central control of oil revenue—with attendant struggles for its distribution—has been among the most serious of Nigeria's problems. See Rotimi T. Suberu, "Nigeria; Dilemmas of Federalism," in Ugo M. Amoretti and Nancy Bermeo, eds., *Federalism and Territorial Cleavages* (Baltimore: Johns Hopkins University Press, 2004), 350–51; V. Adefemi Isumonah, "The Ethnic Language of Rights and the Nigerian Political Community," in Hunter, *Citizenship, Belonging, and Political Community in Africa*, 211–39.

79. A leading figure in the administration of the British Empire, Sir Bartle Frere, thought that Africans could be made into "the subject races of an Imperial mistress, races strong enough to labour and capable of development into worthy integral sections of population in vast and growing empires." Such was one concept of imperial belonging. Lecture from 1878 cited in Saul Dubow, "South Africa and South Africans: Nationality, Belonging, Citizenship," in Robert Ross, Anne Kelk Mager, and Bill Nasson, eds., *The Cambridge History of South Africa Volume 2 1885–1994* (Cambridge: Cambridge University Press, 2011), 25.

80. Klotz, *Migration and National Identity in South* Africa, 150–67; Dubow, "South Africa and South Africans," 17–65. Dubow points to the tensions, most acute since the 1940s, among opponents of white domination in South Africa between those who favored a unitary, nonracial polity, advocates of a multiracial polity that explicitly recognized the collective character of the different communities within South Africa, and an "Africanist" viewpoint that insisted that black Africans should rule Africa. Group-differentiated citizenship was thus one possibility, but since 1994, South African citizenship is in constitutional terms unitary (with relatively strong provincial governments), although the practice of politics has both Africanist and multiracialist aspects.

81. On the politics of basic income support in South Africa and elsewhere, see James Ferguson, *Give a Man a Fish: Reflections on the New Politics of Distribution* (Durham, NC: Duke University Press, 2015); statistic from p. 5. The literature on politics, inequality, and citizenship in South Africa is now vast. See for example Jeremy Seekings and Nicoli Nattrass, *Class, Race, and Inequality in South Africa* (New Haven and London: Yale University Press, 2005); Franco Barchiesi, *Precarious Liberation: Workers, the State, and Contested Social Citizenship in Postapartheid South Africa* (Albany: SUNY Press, 2011); Adam Habib, *South Africa's Suspended Revolution: Hopes and Prospects* (Athens: Ohio

University Press, 2013); Steven Robins, ed., *Limits to Liberation after Apartheid: Citizenship, Governance and Culture in South Africa* (Athens: Ohio University Press, 2005).

82. Tom Lodge, "Neo-Patrimonial Politics in the ANC," *African Affairs* 113 (2014): 1–23. Before 1994, one response to the politics of white domination was that "blacks responded with their own racially embedded ideals." C.R.D. Halisi, *Black Political Thought in the Making of South African Democracy* (Bloomington: Indiana University Press, 1999), 4. This response stood in tension with the ANC's long-standing nonracialism, a tension that is still evident within as well as beyond the party.

83. On citizenship in Eritrea and its diaspora, see Victoria Bernal, *Nation as Network: Diaspora, Cyberspace, and Citizenship* (Chicago: University of Chicago Press, 2014). For a recent installment of the South Sudan debacle, see Jacey Fortin, "Power Struggles Stall South Sudan's Recovery from War," *New York Times*, May 30, 2016. More generally, see Geschiere, *Perils of Belonging*; Morten Bøas and Kevin Dunn, *Politics of Origin in Africa: Autochthony, Citizenship and Conflict* (London: Zed, 2013); and Scott Straus, *Making and Unmaking Nations: War, Leadership, and Genocide in Modern Africa* (Ithaca, NY: Cornell University Press, 2015).

84. One country often cited for maintaining democratic political structures and a reasonable level of public services is Botswana. Its government has evoked the citizenship concept to justify the focusing of resources—in the notable case of the provision on a large scale of drugs for the treatment of AIDS—on its own citizens, not on residents who might be from other countries. Fanny Chabrol, "Soigner les siens: Citoyenneté et imagination nationale au Botswana au temps du SIDA," *Politique Africaine* 136 (2014): 157–77. See also Francis B. Nyamnjoh, "Reconciling 'the Rhetoric of Rights' with Competing Notions of Personhood and Agency in Botswana," in Harri Englund and Francis B. Nyamnjoh, eds., *Rights and the Politics of Recognition in Africa* (London: Zed, 2004), 33–63.

85. Frederick Cooper, *Africa Since 1940: The Past of the Present* (Cambridge: Cambridge University Press, 2002).

86. "Conférence de Presse du 23 Août 1960 par Léopold-Sédar Senghor, Secrétaire Général de UPS," published by Ministère de l'information, de la Presse et de la Radiodiffusion de la République du Sénégal. For discussion, see Cooper, *Citizenship between Empire and Nation*.

87. Since even non-EU migrants legally in a Union country have certain rights, some people argue that European citizenship doesn't add much to an already fragmented notion. But legal—let alone illegal—status is vulnerable to the whims of politics, while European courts have produced a substantial jurisprudence of citizenship that offers protection to European citizens. The courts' role, especially in specifying the contours of social citizenship, is emphasized in Christian Joppke, "The Inevitable Lightening of Citizenship," *European Journal of Sociology* 51 (2010): 9–32, esp. 22.

88. Ulrich Preuss, Michelle Everson, Mathias Koenig-Archibugi, and Edwige Lefebvre, "Traditions of Citizenship in the European Union," *Citizenship Studies* 7 (2003): 3–14, esp. 4.

89. Stefano Giubboni, "European Citizenship and Social Rights in Times of Crisis," *German Law Journal* 15 (2014): 957; Patricia Mindus, "Dimensions of Citizenship," *German Law Journal* 15 (2014): 745. Joppke worries that the process of Europeanizing social citizenship through courts and administration weakens the subjective impact of citizenship. Flexibility and multiple citizenships lessen citizenship's sacral qualities. "Inevitable Lightening," 9–32. Bryan Turner goes further in seeing a diminishment of the citizen's social position relative to that of the legal resident. "We Are All Denizens Now: On the Erosion of Citizenship," *Citizenship Studies* 20 (2016): 679–92.

90. Turkuler Isiksel, *Europe's Functional Constitution: A Theory of Constitutionalism beyond the State* (Oxford: Oxford University Press, 2016), 222; Stéphane Caporal, "L'Europe et le citoyen," in Association Française des Historiens des Idées Politiques, *Sujet and citoyen: Actes du colloque de Lyon (11–12 septembre 2003)* (Aix-en-Provence: Presses Universitaires d'Aix-Marseille, 2004), 441–63, esp. 446–47, 450–51. Peo Hansen and Sandy Brian Hager note the lack of social citizenship at the European level and see instead an "individualized market citizen." In the absence of a social conception, they argue, European leaders have tried to define Europe through a supposed "rootedness in a shared European culture, heritage, history, and civilization." That leaves many people out. *The Politics of European Citizenship: Deepening Contradictions in Social Rights and Migration Policy* (New York: Berghahn Books, 2010), 75.

91. Gregory Mann, *From Empires to NGOs in the West African Sahel: The Road to Nongovernmentality* (Cambridge: Cambridge University Press, 2015).

92. Despite high degrees of internal inequality, rich countries redistribute a considerable portion of their revenues to citizens through their social programs, but, overall, they consign only .35 per cent of national revenue to aid to poor countries. François Bourguignon, *La mondialisation de l'inégalité* (Paris: Seuil, 2012), 79.

93. Weitz, in tracing the history of the concept of self-determination, points to the impossibility of defining conclusively what a people is. The consequences of definitional politics could be emancipatory or the reverse. "Self-Determination," 462–96.

Conclusion: Citizenship in an Unequal World

1. Melissa Lane, *The Birth of Politics: Eight Greek and Roman Political Ideas and Why They Matter* (Princeton, NJ: Princeton University Press, 2014), 185. The image of Janus is also invoked in John Clarke, Kathleen Coll, Evelina Dagnino, and Catherine Neveu, *Disputing Citizenship* (Bristol: Policy Press, 2014), 176.

2. The need to work with these tensions is stressed by two of today's thoughtful political theorists. Seyla Benhabib, "Twilight of Sovereignty or the Emergence of Cosmopolitan Norms? Rethinking Citizenship in Volatile Times," *Citizenship Studies* 11 (2007), 19–36, and *The Rights of Others: Aliens, Residents and Citizens* (Cambridge: Cambridge University Press, 2004), and Jean Cohen, *Globalization and Sovereignty: Rethinking Legality, Legitimacy, and Constitutionalism* (Cambridge: Cambridge University Press, 2012).

3. Engin Isin, "Theorizing Acts of Citizenship," in Isin and Greg Nielsen, eds., *Acts of Citizenship* (London: Zed, 2008), 15–43. Lest one romanticize movements of civil society, it is important to note that they can be demagogic, exclusionary, and violent as well as emancipatory, a point made in regard to Latin America by Joseph Tulchin and Meg Ruthenburg, "Citizens: Made, Not Born," in Tulchin and Ruthenburg, eds., *Citizenship in Latin America* (Boulder, CO: Lynne Rienner, 2007), 281–84.

4. "Citizenship is more than a simple system of inclusion and exclusion, it is powerfully connective." Because it is not inherently tied to ethnicity, religion, race, or class, it contains the possibility of linkages across such divisions—if people have the will to act accordingly. Clarke et al., *Disputing Citizenship*, 164.

5. Rainer Bauböck asks, "Wouldn't it be plausible to assign primary responsibility for 'diversity management' to cities, for social welfare entitlements to states, and for migration policies to the European Union or similar unions of states in other global regions, such as South America?" "Why Liberal Nationalism Does Not Resolve the Progressive's Trilemma: Comment on Will Kymlicka's article "Solidarity in Diverse Societies," *Comparative Migration Studies* 4, 10 (2016), 4.

6. Engin Isin and Peter Nyers see citizenship as vitally needed to struggle against the impositions of global capitalism and "statism." "Introduction: Globalizing Citizenship Studies," in Engin Isin and Peter Nyers, eds., *The Routledge Handbook of Global Citizenship Studies* (London: Routledge, 2014), 6.

7. Evelina Dagnino, "Citizenship in Latin America: An Introduction," *Latin American Perspectives* 30, 2 (2003): 8.

8. On the inconsistent commitment of European institutions to social rights and social protections, see Willem Maas, "European Union Citizenship in Retrospect and Prospect," in Isin and Nyers, *Routledge Handbook of Global Citizenship Studies*, 409–17, esp. 415–16. Alain Supiot sees a global trajectory that goes toward the extension of social rights after World War II, followed by a move in recent decades in the opposite direction, toward treating European citizens as individuals in relation to the market. *The Spirit of Philadelphia: Social Justice vs. the Total Market*, trans. Saskia Brown (London: Verso, 2012).

9. Türküler Isiksel, "Citizens of a New Agora: Postnational Citizenship and International Economic Institutions," in Willem Maas, ed., *Multilevel Citizenship* (Philadelphia: University of Pennsylvania Press, 2013), 184–202.

10. As Jean Cohen points out, sovereignty is a relational concept, involving mutual recognition and "membership in an international society and/or com-

munity of states"—so that there is no inherent contradiction between agreed-upon international standards enforced by international institutions and sovereign states. *Globalization and Sovereignty*, 201. See Patrick Macklem, "Global Poverty and the Right to Development," in *The Sovereignty of Human Rights* (Oxford: Oxford University Press, 2015), 185–223.

11. A high official of the French employers' association (Medef), not noted for its generosity toward the working class, has recently called for a "social Bretton Woods"—that is, for international institutions to respond to people's worry about their social security in parallel to the way international financial institutions protect the economic order. Bernard Spitz, "Le temps est venu d'un nouveau Bretton Woods social," *Le Monde Économie*, 13 January 2017, 7.

12. Simon Turner, "Dans l'oeil du cyclone: Les réfugiés, l'aide et la communauté internationale en Tanzanie," *Politique Africaine* 85 (2002): 29–44, 37 quoted.

INDEX

A NOTE ON THE TYPE

{⟳}

THIS BOOK has been composed in Miller, a Scotch Roman typeface designed by Matthew Carter and first released by Font Bureau in 1997. It resembles Monticello, the typeface developed for The Papers of Thomas Jefferson in the 1940s by C. H. Griffith and P. J. Conkwright and reinterpreted in digital form by Carter in 2003.

Pleasant Jefferson ("P. J.") Conkwright (1905–1986) was Typographer at Princeton University Press from 1939 to 1970. He was an acclaimed book designer and AIGA Medalist.

The ornament used throughout this book was designed by Pierre Simon Fournier (1712–1768) and was a favorite of Conkwright's, used in his design of the *Princeton University Library Chronicle.*